DAEMON IN THE SANCTUARY

DAEMON IN THE SANCTUARY

The Enigma of Homespace Violence

WENDY C. HAMBLET

Algora Publishing
New York

Library of Congress Cataloging-in-Publication Data —

Hamblet, Wendy C., 1949-
    Daemon in the sanctuary: the enigma of homespace violence / Wendy C.
Hamblet.
        pages cm
    Includes bibliographical references.
    ISBN 978-1-62894-036-7 (soft cover: alk. paper) —ISBN 978-1-62894-037-4
(hard cover: alk. paper) —ISBN 978-1-62894-038-1 (ebook)
    1. Violence—Moral and ethical aspects. 2. Family violence. 3. Violence—
Social aspects. I. Title.
    BJ1459.5.H357 2013
    303.6—dc23
                            2013029537

Printed in the United States

TABLE OF CONTENTS

INTRODUCTION

Plato's *Symposium* offers a broad range of poetic and mythical accounts of love, but the dialogue has the overall effect of tearing the god Eros from the heavenly post traditionally assigned him by his eulogists and disciples and resituating him in between the gods and human beings. Eros becomes a daemon. Many might be tempted to interpret love's newly assigned in-between status the same way that Socrates does—as an indication of the mediatory function of love and its elevating power for humans. In this work, however, I propose we take very seriously the demotion of the god from his traditional, highly eulogized status, and explore the less-than-heavenly effects of love that come to be played out and witnessed as violence at the homespace. How can a mediating, connecting force, such as love, be implicated in the pain and tragedy of intimate violence?

Moving from the *Symposium*'s syrupy tributes of the god to the subject of domestic violence appears to be a giant leap, but I will claim here that embroidered romantic ideas about love prepare the initiate poorly for the reality of intimate connection. Poets and philosophers who lead us to believe that love is heaven sent can leave us craving an extreme experience. We crave an earth-shaking, life-altering intrusion on our tranquility as evidence that love is real. Thus the naïve initiate can easily mistake the flutter of the pulse, the quickening of the heart rate, the flush, the confused emotions, and the painful longing as signs of the god's gift. But these are also the signs of fear!

Is it possible that those victims of intimate violence who baffle their family, friends, public protectors, and therapists by returning again and again to the arms of their abuser cannot disentangle the love from the terror, the myth from the reality, the god's gift from the daemonic actuality of their sickened attachment? Perhaps this is the underlying suspicion that causes Plato to place in the mouth of the only non-poetic symposiast, the doctor Eryximachus, a discourse which proposes that love assumes contrary forms; it can be sacred or profane, healthy or sick. The effects of love can be either ruinous or blissful, depending on whether the lovers follow the "fair and heavenly" goddess or the base earthly Aphrodite, "Muse of many songs." It is significant that it is Eryximachus who suggests from the outset of the symposium that the symposiasts "dispense with the services of the flute girl" and drink sensibly of the wine.

CHAPTER ONE. DINNER WITH THE DAEMON

Love is not love
Which alters when it alteration finds,
Or bends with the remover to remove:
O no! it is an ever-fixed mark
That looks on tempests and is never shaken;
(Shakespeare, Sonnet 116)

Hamilton and Cairns' seminal collection of Plato's works introduce the *Symposium* with the sweeping tribute: "It is agreed that the *Symposium* is one of Plato's two greatest dialogues, either greater than the *Republic* or next to it."[1]This praise may have the ring of mere oratory to the ear of the Platonically uninitiated. How could a dialogue treating a topic so apparently frivolous as love warrant first place in the accomplishments of (arguably) the greatest philosopher to have ever written?

The answer to this mystery lies in the delicate and elusive connection between love and justice; it resides in the subtle but relentless way that our loves, those things or people we most value, position us for conduct in the world. Love paints our view of others with the broad strokes of our own desires, causing us to locate in those who are beloved a perfection, a divinity. Loved

---

1 Edith Hamilton and Huntington Cairns, *Plato's Collected Dialogues* (Princeton, New Jersey: Princeton University Press, 1991), p. 526.

ones can appear to us as incapable of wrongdoing. and the integrity of our connection with loved ones can appear invulnerable to time's "bending sickle," a myth confirmed in Shakespeare's most famed love sonnet.[1] Love tints our view of intimates; it purifies and sanctifies their failings and it divinizes their virtues. Love also colors our view of ourselves. Where we feel our love accepted and returned, our self-esteem soars to parallel height with our inflated estimation of the beloved; if I am so worthy to be loved by this god, I am worthy indeed above others.

On the other hand, unreciprocated love can have devastating effects upon the unrequited lover; rejection by the ones we hold most dear can bring shame, agony, and existential ruin. Studies of perpetrators of violent and heinous crimes reveal without fail common histories of neglect and abuse, often occurring in childhood and at the hands of those very loved ones whom nature has stationed to be their protectors and nurturers. Similarly, our loves—our "homegroup"—can situate us to find unloved others—outsiders to the homegroup—as wanting in value and appeal. Strangers and outsiders to the homegroup cannot help but pale in worth beside those to whom we are connected through ties of love. Indeed love can position people to find in those unloved others, outside the sacred circle of their (largely imaginary) commonalities and their (often imaginary) loyalties, the radical other of divinity—the valueless, the undesirable, the monstrous "stranger," paradigmatic figure of the justly feared unknown. Love so colors our vision of the world and configures our understanding of self and others that it can drive us to the point of violent atrocity to protect those who "belong" in our inner, intimate circle of loved ones and to reject those other coarser, baser beings who threaten to contaminate that sacred circle.

The mysterious connection between love and justice lies hidden between the lines of Plato's famed dialogue with which I open this chapter; it is concealed in the shifting interconnections among the varied discourses. Plato artfully weaves the connection between love and justice from the myths and stories and lofty pronouncements he places in the mouths of the poets, the philosopher, the Manitean priestess-seer, the physician and the

---

1 Excerpt from Shakespeare's 116th Sonnet

comic tragedian, and he displays it in the agonized testimony of the unrequited lover who shows up to storm the gracious, rule-bound dinner party. The elusive connection between justice and love resides somewhere "in between" the lines of the speeches, the images of the stories, and the reality of the flesh. The connection cannot be fully captured by any solitary discourse, but it resides in the thematic overlaps among the many voices: the sycophantic speeches in praise of the god of Love; the playful comic-tragic myth tracing love's tragic origin to the arrogance of humans, punished and then pitied by the god; the riddling myth of Eros' birth, espoused by the Mantinean priestess Diotima and recounted by the know-nothing Socrates; and embodied in the living flesh of the tormented and drunken young Alkibiades, a young man of good family and high expectations whose destiny (the reader knows from her "god's eye perch") will be tragically ruined by his unrequited love for Socrates. Let us return once again to that dinner party long ago and witness once again the diverse forms the daemon assumes and the unsavory haunts where he dances, barefoot, duplicitous, and shrewd, seeking out a safe haven where he may safely make his home.

The first mystery that arises in Plato's telling of the love story that is recorded as the dialogue, the *Symposium*, is the question of why the elusive philosopher goes to such labyrinthine lengths to remove the original event from us, the readers. Plato could simply have told us a story, directly recounting the dinner party and offering us the smorgasbord of speeches. But instead he constructs a an elaborate succession of frames, layers of storytelling, that has the practical effect of distancing the reader from the living truth of the dinner party. The frames remind us that we are removed from the event not only by a vast stretch of time, which needs must test the memory of any storyteller, but by a long list of hand-me-down retellings by a series of storytellers. The tale of the dinner party is first introduced to us through the voice and the tested memory of Apollodorus, who recounts the story to Glaucon, the older brother of Plato.

Why does it matter that the story of love is many times removed from our immediate grasp? We know that the distancing is significant because Plato affirms from the outset of the dialogue the importance of presence for the telling of truth. In the

opening lines of the dialogue, Plato has Glaucon ask Apollodorus the telling question: "Were *you yourself present* at that party or
not (172b6)?" (συ αυτος παρεγενου τη συνουσία ταυτη η ου;).
The question of presence straightway reminds the reader of the
importance of accurate witnessing. The question, situated at the
outset of the story, arrives precisely to illuminate the lack of
presence in this case of storytelling. We are straightway made
painfully aware of the immense stretch of absence—the lifetime
of tellings and retellings—that separates the storyteller from the
subject of his speech. Apollodorus admits to Plato's brother that
the dinner party was held "when you and I were in the nursery."
Names have great significance for the ancients and Plato chose
Apollodorus (meaning "gift of Apollo," the far-seeing god who
knows all things clearly) to deliver this truth to us. This contradiction further confirms: the "truth" about love—"the whole
truth and nothing but the truth"—as it is rendered in the *Symposium*, is a tenuous truth at best. It will have traveled a long way to
reach us. Journeys can change everything. Truth can shift along
the way. But even if the truth had been delivered to us firsthand
in a treatise by Plato himself, we must keep in mind that all written tales are untrustworthy, by Plato's own testimony. In the
finale of the *Symposium*'s sister dialogue (also about love), *The
Phaedrus*, writing will be exposed to be as shifty and unreliable as
a "bastard son" who wanders all over the place saying anything
to just anybody.

Across a vast abyss of time, then, the story of the dinner
party reaches us, delivering us an unreliable tale about love. Its
truth has been passed from a priestess, through a philosopher,
and finally through two lovers; it has journeyed from Mantinea
to Athens, and then, by way of Cydathenaeum, back to Athens
again, and finally arrives to our distant shores thousands of years
later. Let us peer through the many frames and give ear to the
succession of storytellers as they bring to presence once again
that dinner party long ago in ancient Athens. Let us see what it
can teach us about love.

The *Symposium* depicts a gathering of friends of varying ages,
reputations, and talents. Set in the home of Agathon, the young,
eloquent rhetorician, the get-together was originally planned
as a drinking party, as a chapter in the ongoing celebration of

Agathon's first tragedy. However, after the friends admit to the various overindulgences of the previous night, the intent of the gathering shifts from another night of drunken frivolity to an elegant, rule-bound, ordered succession of speeches in honor of the god of Love, a subject that arises in response to Phaedrus' disingenuous complaint—that very little reverence has ever been paid to the god. "Not a single poet has ever sung a song in praise of so ancient and so powerful a god as Love" (177ab). The symposium is launched around a complaint that Phaedrus gives in bad faith, as G.R.F. Ferrari notes: love is not simply the name of a god in the Ancient Greek pantheon, but it is also the common name for the emotional attachment between human beings. Phaedrus and the other guests would have been well aware of the long history of famed works of the love poets, from Sappho through Anacreon.[1]

Nonetheless, Phaedrus' fraudulent complaint is passed over without protest from rhetorician, poet, or philosopher. Then Plato straightway strikes us with another surprise: the know-nothing Socrates declares from the start that he has certain knowledge of the "truth" of this subject under inquiry. The reader, like each of the group of symposiasts, must now wait, suffering, wondering, tormented by desire; we must all, like unrequited lovers, endure a series of long, formal speeches, all the while yearning for a resolution to this paradoxical claim by the old philosopher. What exactly does the know-nothing know? And how does he know what he knows? Is Socrates' knowing wise, given his definition recorded in the *Apology* (20c): human wisdom resides in knowing that we cannot know.

The first speech is given by Phaedrus, the young sensualist whom we already know to be a deceiver from his fraudulent complaint that secures the topic for the speeches. We will meet Phaedrus again in the sister dialogue on love that bears his name, where he will be lounging with Socrates on the banks of the river in an enchanted spot outside the city, exploring love once again. Phaedrus' speech at the dinner party calls is a traditional eulogy. It calls upon ancient authorities to witness its truth claims: Hesiod, Homer, Acusilaus, Father Parmenides, and

---

1 See G. R. F. Ferrari, "Platonic Love" in *Cambridge Companion to Plato* (Cambridge: Cambridge University Press, 1992), pp. 248-276.

Aeschylus help Phaedrus to illuminate the god's lofty stature as the archaic source of greatest good and happiness for humans.

Pausanias, the lover of the poet Agathon, then follows Phaedrus' eulogy, only to undermine the young lover's simple, unambiguous discourse about love's simple, unambiguous goodness. Pausanias declares Eros to be of shifting kinds and shifting effects. It can be earthly or heavenly "according to the goddess in whose company [his] work is done" (180e). In itself, love is neither good nor bad; it is amoral and has no virtue in himself. His virtue or lack thereof comes through his actions. Love is good only when he exercises his noble, heavenly bearing, "when he moves us to love nobly" (181a). Love's dual parentage affords the son a shifting nature, and his works, his effects, vary accordingly, as he descends from his two goddess-mothers—the elder heavenly Aphrodite, the Uranian sprung motherless from King Zeus' head; and the younger earthly Aphrodite, Pandemus, daughter of Zeus and Dione.

Love's nature, then, reflects this conflicted parentage, so he can at times perform heavenly deeds, but at other times his works will be base and ignoble, governed by vulgar passions. Love's effects vary in moral quality with the individual concrete situation; his desires may be directed at the body or the soul, he may behave graciously or badly, and he may target his affection on the shallowest object or pursue an edifying favorite. Pausanias concludes: "the outcome of each action depends upon *how* it is performed" (181a). Significantly, for this lover, heavenly love is all man; it admits of no feminine qualities, but has a "vigorous and intellectual bent" (181d).

Next the physician Eryximachus speaks, since Aristophanes, next on the schedule, was taken by a fit of hiccups. He sticks with the dualistic understanding of love introduced by Pausanias but he inflates Pausanias' dichotomy to the cosmic level, linking the noble and ignoble principles with notions of health and illness. For Eryximachus, these principles hold sway across the entire cosmos, keeping the universe in balance or throwing the cosmic equilibrium into havoc. Love is the principle that balances or imbalances the human landscape and the "brute and vegetable creations" (186a) as well.

Aristophanes, his bearing now reclaimed after the annoying

fit of hiccups, offers a speech that wonders at the contingencies of fleshy existence. His tale composes a tragic myth that paradoxically serves as comic relief from the serious formal eulogies that preceded him. His tale tells of human beings in an original state, as funny round little arrogant creatures who had the cheek to roll up Mount Olympus and set upon the gods. Zeus repaid their fateful *hybris*, always regarded among the Greeks as the most scandalous human failing, by tearing the creatures asunder, splitting them into broken, sad, little half-creatures, no longer able to arrogantly roll anywhere. The comic poet declares matter-of-factly: "[Zeus] cut them all in half just as you and I might chop up sorb apples for pickling, or slice an egg with a hair" (190de). But the story does not end at this tragic point. Ultimately, Zeus takes pity on the naughty beings and has his brother Hephaestus rearrange and re-forge their broken bodies so that they can latch onto each other in sexual union and achieve temporary respite from their pain and yearning. The conclusion of the comic's tale of love is an uproarious scene of chaotic, awkward bumbling, as the lovers run wildly about, "questing and clasping" at each other in a desperate but ridiculous hunt for that single unique other half that will make each feel whole again. But the funny conclusion is not the last word in the comic's tale; Aristophanes ends the story with a cold and haunting warning from the king of the gods: "If I have any more trouble with them, I shall split them up again, and they'll have to hop about on one [leg]" (190d).

The comic-tragic veil of *mythos* is then punctured, as Agathon returns the symposium to oratory mode and lets launch a sermon of syrupy praise, heaping honor after honor on the god of love. From the tormented *pathos* of Aristophanic loss, the god is raised again to his divine station, above the fray of mundane existence and the troubling contingencies of broken flesh and tormented soul. Now Eros is extolled as the most blessed of the gods—the youngest, the most delicate, the most tender, the most genius, the most righteous, the most temperate of deities, never violent, always affable, elegant and gracious. At the close of this sugary oration, Socrates loses patience with the sycophantic monologue. He punctures Agathon's inflated bubble of praise with the denunciation: "The truth, it seems, is the last thing that the successful eulogist cares about."

At long last, Socrates' turn arrives and we, like impatient lovers, lean from the edges of our seats to catch a glimpse that will answer the mystery raised by Socrates' claim to certain knowledge on this topic. Like Aristophanes, Socrates refuses the general form of speech of the evening. Eschewing mere tribute, he casts his "certain truth" about love in the shadowy imagery of myth. But, testimony to Plato's genius, Socrates' story about love sounds suspiciously familiar. Fragments of the many accounts offered by the previous speakers resonate through Socrates' tale, while other crucial elements of their tales are conspicuous in the absence. Socrates begins by drawing from Agathon the admission (resonant with Aristophanes' myth) that love cannot admit of any of the hyperbolic features that he (Agathon) and the other eulogists had heaped upon him, because love, whose presence can always be detected by the evidence of longing and yearning, cannot be associated with a superabundance of anything. Love's pining, lusting, aching qualities can only be associated with lack.

Because of this lack, reasons Socrates, love cannot be counted among the gods. Gods are fully happy, beautiful, self-sufficient, and wise; they want for nothing. However, love is not a lowly mortal, either; so he must be some other kind of creature, a being that stands somewhere between the two. Eros is a daemon or messenger caught between the two realms. This offers Socrates a convenient transition to Diotima's myth, which Socrates then proceeds to recount. The mystery is solved: Socrates still knows nothing, but he has the testimony of the priestess that allows him a glimpse of the truth.

Socrates reports Diotima's tale. Love was born on the day of Aphrodite's birth, which explains why love yearns eternally after the beautiful. Eros is a male but, unlike Pausanias' "vigorous and intellectual" male love, he is hardly unambiguously gracious and dignified; nor is he faithfully focused on honorable intellectual pursuits. This ambiguity is readily understandable, when Diotima recounts the daemon's heritage. Eros was conceived through the wiles of the vagrant goddess *Penia* (whose name means Want, Need, or Poverty), who had come begging at the door during a drinking party of the gods. In the garden of Zeus, she came upon the god *Poros* (whose name means Plenty, Abundance, Resource, or Cunning, literally "a passageway through"), who had passed out from an overindulgence of nectar. *Poros'* own celebrated resourcefulness drowned in drunken stupor, *Penia*'s cunning neediness got the better of him and so was the daemon brought to conception.

Thus, continues Socrates, love is claimed, after his father, to be a mighty hunter, gallant, impetuous and artful. But the reader cannot wonder at this tribute, since there seems an obvious absence of paternal influence in Socrates' description of the daemon: love cannot find himself a safe refuge; he remains homeless and ever wandering, sleeping in doorways and under the stars. Harsh, arid, and barefoot, Eros wanders about, longing after the wisdom and excellence and beauty that can never be his; he remains unrequited in all his desires.

At this point in the tale of Love, the story takes an abrupt shift to the subject of love's effects in the world. Socrates launches this subject from the priestess' categorical statement: all men are lovers of the beautiful and the good. The most beautiful and good are immortal, so lovers, whether mortal or daemonic, have as their primary target immortality, which they seek in the only way open to them, in products that endure the test of time, in creations that outlast them. Love wants to live forever but, this being impossible, the lover throws herself into the future in fecundity: "To love is to bring forth upon the beautiful, both in body and in soul" (206b). Socrates reports Diotima's truth:

> We are all of us prolific, Socrates, in body and soul and...our nature urges us to procreation. We cannot be quicked by ugliness but only by the beautiful...ugliness is at odds with the divine, while beauty is in perfect harmony.

It is critically important that love remains staunchly focused on beautiful ends and brings forth only good effects. Diotima warns Socrates against the love that does not keep faith with the beautiful: depression, repulsion, pain, and social withdrawal are signals that love is bound up with ugly, base, ignoble things. Diotima declares:

> When [procreation] meets with ugliness, it is over-

come with heaviness and gloom, and, turning away, it shrinks into itself and is not brought to bed, but continues to labour under its painful burden. (206d)

Beauty's importance broadly underscored and love's futuristic disposition decided, Diotima's discourse on Love concludes with the construction of a great ladder of love's creative products, a ladder ascending from the particular to the universal. From the love of a single beautiful body, the lover then climbs to an appreciation of the beauty of all beautiful bodies. On the lover climbs to the love of beauties of the soul, then the beauty of laws and institutions, then to the love of every kind of knowledge, and finally to the love of philosophy, "an open sea of beauty, seed of the most fruitful discourse," where the lover "reap[s] a golden harvest" (210d). At the summit of love's ladder, the lover embraces at last the one single form of Beauty—the everlasting, eternal wholeness in which all beautiful things participate. This is the very soul of Beauty "unsullied, unalloyed, and freed from the mortal taint that haunts the frailer loveliness of flesh and blood" (211e).

At this lofty moment when the truth of love has been revealed as procreation of all sorts of beautiful products of body and mind, the symposiasts could easily close the inquiry, raise a final toast to Beauty divine, and like Descartes, retire to the fireside, don warm slippers and robe, and rest comfortable in the sure knowledge that they know all the secrets that are to be known about love. But Plato does *not* allow the bliss-struck lovers to close the book on love's truth. Instead, he chooses to add a final scene to this story, a scene that bursts the magical spell of that blissful, ethereal image; a sudden, raucous earthly reality shatters the enchanted moment: the love-torn, heartsick Alkibiades, drunk, tormented, aching, longing for a fulfillment that never will be. Alkibiades' confession of his utter despair reminds us what it is *really* like to be in love down here in the hollows of the earth. Throwing us back to Aristophanes' tragic account of the love, the desperate lover reminds us of the fragility that characterizes *human* love, the agony of earthly yearning, its fleshy, bloody, teary, tormenting aspect, so far from heavenly bliss.

The crucial thing about love, which has been missed by the young sensualist Phaedrus, the old philosopher, and even the priestess, as she erected her lofty ladder to the heavens, was already diagnosed by the doctor Eryximachus in his warning about love's baser earthly form—love can bring about an imbalance that is dangerous for our health. The tragic-comic poet too identified the danger and captured it in his imagery of sad, torn little creatures, questing and clasping after that elusive singular other half quite impossible to find. The terrible risk of earthly love is confirmed in the tortured example of the lovesick Alkibiades: lovers are not interchangeable. Diotima has deceived us! We cannot without tragic consequences abandon one beloved and step easily up the ladder of love to reach for the next, loftier beauty.

When earthly love is lost, the lover is left torn and fragmented; no substitute, no matter how beautiful, can ease the pain or step into the place of the beloved. In anguished and suffering longing, Aristophanes' hopelessly questing lovers *cannot* "bring forth upon the beautiful" any more than the ruined lover, Alkibiades, can forget his loss and happily move on. Their tragedies remind us that when love is lost, everything valuable in life can collapse as well. Plato knows—as does the reader—that Alkibiades' torment will open upon a future far from the noble ends of Diotima's ladder; shame, deception, treachery, and finally bloody murder are the products of this lover's suffering.

Poros may be a resourceful father and *Penia* proved herself no less crafty than he, but the victims of their offspring daemon, Eros, cannot always find their way to the plentiful abundance of happiness and beautiful works that the father's name implies and that Diotima's ladder promised. Love *does* have to do primarily with a future, with the desire for beautiful ends, for the joining of torn pieces of lives and flesh, and sometimes even for vigorous and intelligent fulfillment. But not all of love's ends are beautiful, not all of love's yearnings wholesome and heavenly. The crafty priestess, archetypally riddling in her truth, conveniently omits a good many of love's common products from her ladder of noble creations.

In all too many earthly cases, love ruins its supplicants, destroys their dreams and their hope for the future. As the comic, the doctor, and the young warrior-politician Alkibiades indicate, love lost is not merely the slow drying up of the river of passion; it can be a turning of its blistering tide, a torrential flood of misdirected desire that carries away all courage and reason. Love may politely excuse himself and slip from the garden of the gods, but his absence can remain tenderly, sorely ever-present for the abandoned lover. The wound of incompleteness remains gaping, bloody, and raw. This is not beauty (*kalos*) but its opposite, *aiskuros*, grotesqueness, ugliness, shamefulness. As Diotima warned, ugliness is always "at odds with the divine," so when love fails and leaves ugly, festering wounds, the goddess of Beauty turns away, drawing up her splendid ladder that promises eternity to love's believers.

In the *Symposium*, love's yearning leads up a ladder whose every lofty rung brings increasing beauty, tranquility, and wholeness, and these products are mirrored in the soul of the lover as she ascends ever closer to bliss and divinity. There is little doubt that love can fulfill itself in beautiful ends, when the climb is smooth and the lovers climb together. But it is important to remember that Plato is ever a Greek and for the Greeks, ends always unfold logically from origins; origins tell the truth about things and prefigure their destinies. Love is born of deceit and neediness, and consequently he spends his days wandering about as a barefoot orphan. Carefree and homeless, he sleeps around wherever he can find a bed—in a stranger's doorway or on the grass under the stars. Well we might wonder whether such a vagabond is capable of settling down and being faithful to a single beloved or sticking around when the sticking gets tough and the thrill of adventure has waned.

Love is a wild and wandering being. To know his earthly aspect, we cannot climb above the troubling flux of earthly life, but we must instead follow the ladder downward into the depths of the everyday. We must consider love's ugly products, where the goddess has turned away.

Socrates claimed that love is the one thing he knows about with certainty. But has the philosopher missed the mark of truth by listening only to the riddling seer, and dismissing the tragic warnings of the comic poet and the fleshy testimony of the wounded lover? It seems that of all the discourses on Love, the doctor Eryximachus may have come closest to the truth: Love involves contradictory things. When love is heavenly, its products are beautiful and a credit to their creators, but when love turns base and produces ugliness, only misery and shame are mirrored in their makers' souls. Love is *really* about Socrates and Agathon, beauty and bliss, eloquence and goodness. But it is also *really* about tortured absence, the tragic-comedy of existence, mourning and irrevocable loss. Diotima's ladder fails to account for all of love's children. Love can wander many directions—to the heavens or into the hell realms. Perhaps this is what Socrates is trying to tell Agathon and Aristophanes, at daybreak the morning after the dinner party, when he wonders whether tragedy and comedy might emerge from the same creative source (*Sym.* 223d).

CHAPTER TWO. THE GOD FALLS FROM THE HEAVENS

The eulogists report that Love is a blessed and divine gift that, once acquired, renders its disciples once and for all gentler, kinder, more beautiful human beings. Love is figured by many to be the magic ingredient of human fulfillment which completes the fragmented being; it is the magical substance that enters the homespace and turns a house into a home. However, as we have seen in the speeches, myths, and human examples of the *Symposium*, love is not simply a god, as the eulogists claim in their syrupy flatteries. Love is also the name we give to the powerful force that tears people and communities apart. As the comic Aristophanes depicts in his myth, love is a blind, driving force that tears the helm from our hands, pushes us all over the place, and leaves us rudderless and lost, seeking and grasping at any port of call in a futile quest for a lost destination.

Religionists, musical lyricists, and poets tell us that all we need is love to heal the world. But love is no sure answer to the violence that floods the globe and seeps into the homespace; indeed often love is the cause of societal violence, fast growing to epidemic proportions under the forces of late capitalism, rather than the solution to violence. Love is not an unambiguously good thing, an inalienable blessing to all it touches. Love has many faces and some of them are ugly and cruel and mean. What matters for peace and tranquility in our communities is not that people love each other, but that they treat each other with kindness and respect.

Within our homes too, the important thing is not *that* the inmates love each other but *how* they love each other. If love is nurturing, supportive, confidence-inspiring, and reliable in all homely weather, it prepares inmates to fly out into the wider world with self-confidence, trust, and grace. But when love is stifling, possessive, obsessive, frantic, fearful, and exclusionary, inmates are poorly schooled for life, both in their homes and in their community.

Plato insists that because the gods serve as primary exemplars for human conduct, stories about them should only portray them as doing good.[1] It is significant that Plato repeats this injunction over and over in the dialogue he devotes to justice. It is also significant that in the *Symposium* where he stages the old master's "truth" about love, he has Socrates cite a semi-divine source—a priestess is a medium herself!—to dispel the myth that love is divine. Love is stationed ontologically in-between the human and divine realms and serves as a medium between the two realms. Love's parents are both divine, and he is conceived in the garden of the gods, so well we might ask about his demotion in Socrates' story. We may assume that Plato assigns to love its in-between ontological status in this dialogue, because the gods, in his description, must be dependable; we must be able to count upon them to behave themselves. However, Eros is by its very nature unpredictable and capricious. Socrates' myth depicts why love's character is thus flawed: love issues from parentage of radically incongruous characters and carries the traits of both. On the one hand, Love inherits neediness and poverty from his mother, *Penia* ("Need" or "Bereft of Resources"), while quite opposite features are bequeathed to him by his father, *Poros* ("Plenty" or "Resourcefulness"). However, the ambiguity encoded in the daemon's nature goes well beyond the contradictory traits of his parents, because plenty of ambiguity characterizes *each* of these parents as well, since the father, known for his cleverness and resourcefulness, was easily

---

1 Plato, *Republic* 2.377, & ff, 3.391c & ff; 4.408c; c.f. *Laws* 12.941b.

outwitted by the supposedly resource-less mother on the occasion of the conception.

Contrary to Phaedrus' disingenuous complaint that launches
the speeches in the *Symposium*, poets, bards, and philosophers
throughout history have always dedicated to Eros a wealth of
flattering encomiums, attributing to the god the highest ranking
among all coveted blessings. In their myriad tributes and homages, the eulogists applaud Eros as the source of unparalleled bliss.
But these unambiguous tributes only tell half the tale about the
daemon. They leave out the other half of the truth that we recognize in the fragmented agony of Aristophanes' split creatures
and witness in the tormented, lovesick Alkibiades. When Eros
is not behaving himself, as the gods are required to do, he can be
the source of unparalleled suffering.

The poets who heap praises upon Eros may sometimes acknowledge the sufferings caused by love, but they tend to interpret the pains of love positively—as evidence of love's intensity.
Love songs moan of arduous yearning, mad cravings, and impris-
onment by ravenous desires, tortured separations, and the wild
despair of Love's loss. Among the vast catalogue of Love's color-
ful symbolism, images of pain and suffering figure prominently
among the daemonic blessings. Despite the abundance of painful
imagery, Love's eulogists do not question, as Plato does in the
Symposium, the god's purely divine status and his worthiness of
pious devotion.

Religions and philosophies of the Eastern tradition, however, ever focused on cultivating the tranquil and peaceable life,
advocate a path that seems to lie far from Eros' rocky, if ethereal,
climes. Instead, the path of non-attachment is promoted, solidly
grounded on the precept of non-harming (*ahimsa*) and driven
by a different sort of caring, the broader affects of compassion
(*karuna*) and loving-kindness (*metta*) extended across the entire family of living creatures in general, without distinguishing
what is "mine" from what does not belong. In no Eastern belief
system is this more true than in the Buddhist tradition, a creed
often called "the religion of no religion" for its dedicated emphasis upon peaceable lifestyle to the utter neglect of metaphysical
abstraction.

The essential Buddhist Dharma, contained in The Four Noble Truths, offers a stark formula for overcoming the suffering that is an inevitable aspect of clinging love: since (1) life is suffering (*dukkha*) and (2) suffering is caused by craving, (3) the way to end suffering is to extinguish desire by abandoning all attachment and (4) adhering to a strict regimen of ethical practices, known as The Eightfold Path. The fourth noble truth may seem a gratuitous and onerous widow unnecessary to the argument that precedes it, but this multifaceted guidebook for the happy, tranquil life betrays the manifold ways that "attached" lovers can go astray when blinded by their craving.

The Fourth Noble Truth indicates that one has a stark choice to make in deciding the kind of life one wishes to live and the kind of human being one seeks to become: one can choose the rocky path of needy, clinging love for the singular, cherished object, with its passionate highs, its agonizing lows, and its inventory of moral pitfalls, or one can choose the simple noble life, with its antipathy for attachment and dependency, its monkish attention to right conduct of life, and its broader mission of caring compassion and loving kindness to the neglect of particular attachments.

My childhood experiences provided me early insight into the difficulties of fiery romantic love. I was second-born in a family of eight children, tumbling up together in a big household under the exacting rule of an English war-bride mother. None of us kids harbored the slightest doubt about the fierceness of the love that bound our hot-blooded, volatile mother and our gentle, yielding, devoted Canadian father. Even mere children unschooled in matters of romance could readily see the passion undergirding the heated arguments, the caustic insults, the agonizing silences, and the occasional cruel betrayals that shook our home and undermined our sense of security. Infrequent and meaningless as these troubled times were in the grander scheme of our long and happy childhoods, the combative spectacles endured during our formative years left each of us children painfully distrustful and cynical of love's unmixed purity. We learned the hard truth early: passionate love is no guarantor against misery and malice but a frequent facilitator thereof.

The poets would argue that anything worth having is worth the pain it costs. "For surely all great things carry with them the risk of a fall and . . . fine things are hard," Plato tells in the *Republic* (497d). Spinoza echoes this fortifying platitude in the closing words of his *Ethics*: "All things excellent are as difficult as they are rare." It may be the case that some loves are true examples of those fine things which poets and philosophers praise—excellent and difficult, but worth every moment of struggle. But I suspect such excellent loves to be, as Spinoza states, as rare as they are difficult, while the vast majority of relations that people name after the god are far from excellent, tortuously difficult, and all too commonly found.

In this work, I propose to challenge the syrupy eulogies spun over these thousands of years, strip the rose-colored lenses from our view of love, track the effects of his fiery presence at the home site, explore the notion of sacrifice (attributed to him by the priestess) as it shows up at the homespace, capture the daemon's dark alter-aspect that raises its ugly head when the doors of the domicile slam closed, and finally turn to the therapists and the Buddhists for advice on how to tame the crafty daemon and heal the love-sickened heart. I warn the reader in advance: the revelations of this book may be discomfiting. Those who feel themselves safely enveloped in the comforting veil of love's mythology will resent having that veil drawn aside and the god's daemonic aspect exposed. But those who have suffered the faithlessness, the cruelty, and the wantonness of love will recognize the daemon laid bare here, stripped of his divine epithets.

CHAPTER THREE. THE AMBIGUOUS ROOTS OF HOMESPACE LOVE

We have seen that the know-nothing Socrates makes a shocking revelation in the *Symposium*. He asserts that love is the one thing about which he knows the truth. The truth, received from the priestess Diotima, is that Eros is no god, but only a half-god, a daemon caught between heaven and earth. Eros is a mediator between the two realms, carrying human supplications *upwards* and delivering *downward* divine commands and rulings. Far from perfect and self-sufficient, the daemon is paradoxical fusion of qualities: he is a young, needy, barefoot wanderer and an ancient, resourceful trickster. He delivers to mortals divine blessings but also the gods' commands and curses, and he returns to the heavens with the prayers and entreaties of the mortals below, armed only with artifices and deceptions for negotiating on their behalf.

So the daemon, despite providing to mortals a critical link with the divine, turns out to be an ambiguous ally who delivers to the lower realm a mixed bag of consequences. He reminds us of Prometheus, another ambiguous ally of humans, whose "gift" of fire, stolen from the gods, brought warmth and tool-making and formidable weaponry, but also brought down the wrath of Zeus upon human beings. We are bound to invite the daemon into our homes when he comes knocking, because he tempts us with heavenly connection. But when the messages he carries turns out to be a curse, our homes and our crops can be laid to waste by our ambiguous visitor.

How we handle the daemon when he enters our lives can be determinative of the degree to which we live full, well-spirited, flourishing lives outside the portals of the home, because the home is the cradle that nurtures our human unfolding, sets the moral trajectory of our life path, and prepares us for the unique karmic adventure that awaits us. How we love those in close proximity to us is an algorithm for our broader bonding experience. Intimate love can configure our capacity for compassion for non-intimates—neighbors and strangers. We practice our caring in the homespace, before we carry it out into the world.

This is the key to unlocking the mystery of the superior rating of the *Symposium* in relation to other of Plato's many dialogues, its equal or greater stature with the very important ten books of the great work, the *Republic*, Plato's master work about justice. Justice may be, as it is repeatedly confirmed in the opening book of the *Republic*, the "definitive" human excellence, but justice and love have deep connections that are grounded in the homespace experience. For Plato, justice too is a median virtue, standing above other common virtues but below the Great Sun of the Good. Both love and justice find their primary site of nurture in the homespace, before they extend themselves out into the city, and finally across the broader human world. From the moment of our conception, the primary task of homespace education is to teach the young how to love others rightly, how to treat other people justly. Justice, the virtue that defines human excellence, joins courage with reason and self-restraint, while Love, the medium, is the umbilical cord that attaches our delicate mortal flesh to the eternity of divine perfection.

Philosophers of the ancient world warn of the fragility of human goodness. We are faulty frail creatures, they tell us, driven by self-interest, fevered flesh, and wanton desires, always quarreling amongst ourselves and grasping after individual interests. Anthropologists confirm the philosophers' ill opinions of our breed, reporting that the earliest humans, huddled around fires in caves and hollows, seeking shelter from the cruel elements and in hiding from fierce predators, were always ready to turn on each other and on outgroups. Indeed, the most brutal and bloody practices, from ritual murder-sacrifices of human and animal victims to torture and expulsion of those who were markedly different, characterized the advent of human communal life. Violence, argue the anthropologists, is not simply an occasional visitor to the homespace; it is an integral force and founding member of the household. Vicious intraspecies atrocities began with the first human clan and increased in direct proportion to the size and power of the growing community.

People tend to feel an immediate connection with people who are like them; the scientists call this phenomenon "pseudokinship." We like those like who are like us, we seek out opportunities to mix with them, and the more time we spend with them, the more in turn we mirror the traits of each other—the more we become like each other. When we examine the complex ritual lives of the earliest human communities, we find a rich palette of violent rituals for sorting and ranking members of the group, suppressing difference within the fold, carving out a sense of belonging and common identity, and distinguishing the ingroup from outgroups. Rituals of human and animal torture, mutilation, and murder sacrifice were pervasively practiced among the earliest human clans. Anthropologists' accounts of these rituals help us to trace how violence came to be normative and pervasive in many societies today. First these violent rituals are called upon for purposes of ranking and ordering the members within the group, so everybody is cast in her proper role and unique place within the hierarchy of power. Then violent rituals extend to configure the modes of interaction between members of the ingroup, as goods and power are distributed according to the core "messages" of power-distribution, communicated in violent rituals. Rituals of violence do not simply structure identities by assigning social place; their sorting and ordering power resides in their unequal distribution of the benefits of the society. Violent rituals of inclusion and exclusion determine who has preferential access to the goods of the society, including power and social status.

Thus political and economic systems are born of violent rituals. Long after the society has become "civilized" and open violence has been suppressed and sublimated, the ritual violence that configured political and economic power in the earliest days of the group's formation continues to function behind the scenes at a subliminal level to keep people in their places and to keep the society "ordered." Over time the violent rituals that include some and exclude others become ever more subtle and concealed, but they remain dogged in their persistence, as they continue to elevate the historically fortunate to the echelons of power and keep the historically unfortunate at the base of the social ladder. Anthropologists who study archaic human rituals demonstrate that violence, from subtle slights to cruel assaults to elimination, has been a longstanding member of the loving homespace from the time that our species first gathered in caves and hunched around a communal fire.

The earliest peoples in simple clans formed a sense of identity and established communal solidarity over against out-groups through starkly clear and radically polarized identifications of the parts of their world. They shared an appreciation of their common features and named these "good," and on the basis of this starkly clear goodness, they were predisposed to find difference, both within their worlds and in the surrounding environment, as contrary to the good—as evil. Within this oversimplified and dichotomous worldview, early humans most certainly valued, and nurtured in their young, the virtues that proved most conducive to the continuance of their group—leading them to safe dwelling places and bountiful hunting grounds, protecting them from the rigors of nature and roving bands of enemies, partaking in highly perilous hunts against large carnivores, and possibly raiding neighboring clans who threatened them or challenged their hunting territory. This means that hypermasculine or militaristic virtues, such as bravery, loyalty, endurance, cunning, resourcefulness, quick-wittedness, and blind obedience to authority were valued above others, though certainly the more womanly virtues of home, such as cooking, medicinal know-how, and child-rearing and fire-tending expertise, commanded respect as well.

In times of peace and prosperity, polarized identifications (good and evil; friend and foe; sacred and profane) would fall to the background of identity work and people would be more accepting of those internal members who were a little different from themselves, and they could probably afford to be more generous toward strangers who showed up on their territorial doorsteps. However, at times when the socio-historical world was shifting and societal harmony was shaken by food shortage, war, disease, or natural disaster, communal integrity could quickly become undermined.

At such troubled times, early communities easily reverted to the radically polarized view of the world and straightway scanned the conceptual landscape to locate the source of the crisis in someone or something different, appearing on the horizon of the lifeworld. The same ordering mechanism that allowed the home group to think of itself as valuable and worth preserving configured the different as alien and evil. This polarized understanding of the world—us versus them—was always ready at hand to explain social chaos in a way that pulled the ingroup together over against an alien threat. The distinction between home group and alien paralleled the distinction between health and disease; the outgroup (or outliers within the home group) infected the good community as a disease, creeping in from the outside to violate their purity and sicken.

The notion of infection of the sacred community, by the profane forces of evil external to it, served the community on several levels. It unequivocally exculpated the home group of implication in the social chaos while it also became the occasion for the renewed solidification of the community, whose members were at each other's throats moments before but then clung together in solidarity against the insidious infection. Furthermore, when the home space is understood as compromised or under threat, another favorable opportunity opens: the occasion is created for the emergence of ingroup heroes. Noble qualities are called forth from the menfolk to make their women proud and provide moral examples for the young, and legends of heroic prowess in battles against the threatening evils enhance the self-image of the entire group, by providing tales of glory that will serve group pride and identity for generations to come.

According to many anthropologists, sacrifice of different ingroup members or countercultural rejection rituals (war) against external neighbors have been practiced so long and so extensively across the landscape of human time (Girard would say "universally") that nurture has become nature. Demonization of difference has become embedded in human nature and encoded in human genes, predisposing people generations and millennia later to blame strangers for their troubles and to opt for hyper-aggressive responses to the vicissitudes of life.

The irony of all of this is that strangers are only in the rarest instances the cause of other people's troubles. Statistics confirm that in every society, ingroups tend almost exclusively to prey upon ingroups. Far more likely than a stranger's attack is the likelihood that you will be kicked, beaten, punched, knifed, raped or even killed in your own home or the home of a close connection, at the hands of someone you know intimately. We readily fear strangers and suspect ill intent from anyone who is different from us, when social scientific evidence attests unequivocally that we ought to have the greatest fear for those who are just like us!

Why does the overwhelming statistical data not convince us to beware of intimates rather than strangers? Numbers on surveys are not *humanly* convincing; they do not speak directly to our phenomenological experience of the world. Phenomenology, as a philosophical methodology, does not even aspire to ascertaining absolute or empirical truth. The phenomenologist aspires to faithfully articulate the lived experience of a subject, confronted by particular experiences and certain aspects of the world. A phenomenological account of the experience of home will reveal that home is generally experienced as a mixed reality. On the one hand, home is a place where the expectation of security and comfort is primary, and this includes the predisposition to find others "like me"—with shared values, practices, and beliefs about what constitutes good and evil, normalcy and deviance. To the familiar, the home offers warmth and welcome. By extension, home is experienced as the site that must, by definition, have an open aspect. It must be generous and welcoming. It must open its doors and windows onto the human community, extend the hand of friendship to neighbors, and offer respite to the weary passer-by.

On the other hand, the more that the homespace is open, the riskier its orientation. How can the home promise security and nurturance to its inmates if it is irresponsible about its doors and windows? The perimeters of the domicile must be well guarded and the comings and goings at the entrances must be constantly surveyed, if the inmates are to be freed from the fear of harm that will erode their happiness and risk their continuance. Security is a fundamental aspect of the home, and it is highly visible under the phenomenologist's gaze. We *feel* that our homes must be safe before they are prosperous and generous to others.

The dual aspects of home—security and welcome—dictate that home is a fundamentally conflicted site, with conflicted goals, conflicted missions, conflicting views of the human world beyond its doors, and conflicted values for achieving its goals, and it will promote conflicted virtues in its indwellers. In times of peace and plenty, the border patrols can relax and the home's abundance can overflow onto its neighbors and passers-by. But in times of economic scarcity and social unrest, when the home feels threatened, the security aspect will take prominence and, as in the state during siege or martial law, xenophobia will eclipse the home's generous aspect, and inmates will become disposed to violence—toward the supposedly mutinous within and the supposedly threatening without.

The two aspects of home are reflected at every level of identity where people carve out their unique sense of self. In the family, in the religious community, in the ethnic subgroup and on the state level, conflicting forces battle for supremacy over which of the Janus faces will take prominence. Since aggression rears its ugly head in times of scarcity, we might expect less class conflict in the developed and prosperous societies of the Western world. Experts in conflict theory, however, note quite the opposite features. They highlight the tendency of industrial societies to produce alienated, isolated, hyper-competitive individuals who seek personal gain over communal benefits, care little about their neighbors, and are quick to abandon even their familial ties and social responsibilities in pursuit of private gain.

Industrialized consumerist society leaves much to be *humanly* desired, but people are not generally worried by the dehumanizing world outside their homes because they genuinely believe that the private realm can exist radically separated from the public world of politics and business. The home counts upon a magical ingredient to hold the family intact—love. Indeed many people recommend that the world at large can be cured of its many ills if only a way can be found to export that magical ingredient across the human landscape. All we need is love, croon the romantics, and the world will be as one happy family. But the fact that violence resides largely at the homespace suggests that the wonder drug of love must have some deep internal flaws of its own. To locate the moral faultlines in the ontological glue that turns a house into a home and a home into a battlefield, we will turn to the philosopher's daemon to see what mischief he is likely to stir up.

Finally, we will turn our attention to the task of dealing with the harsh reality of home and consider some new curative approaches for the violence that infects the homespace. We will investigate how a new generation of practitioners is intervening in violent homes to help people better understand and manage the cycles of violence that mount among them and tear their families apart.

CHAPTER FOUR. THE AMBIGUOUS LOGIC OF THE HOMESPACE

No matter how diligently our parents instilled in us a sense of responsibility, no amount of elementary groundwork can adequately prepare us for the shocking weight of responsibility that dawns upon us quite suddenly as we transition from carefree young adult to parent. The experience of becoming a parent, as steeped in joy as it is, is fraught with the overwhelming sense of responsibility for another life, a frail and fragile spark of life, barely begun but always so close to death in its utter inability to fend for itself. The transition is a stunning one, and particularly so with the firstborn.

People who have slept well all their lives and spent their waking hours relatively free from dread suddenly, in their new role as parents, find themselves hypervigilant, attuned to every sound in the night, every movement in their home and on their street. People never before prone to suspiciousness or pessimism find themselves looking at their friends less confidently and their neighbors more exactingly. Even their own parents are suddenly called into question as trustworthy around the new offspring, as parents review the secret tragedies of their own upbringing and plot to spare their children the disappointments they suffered and the neuroses they continue to bear.

Suddenly the world is an altogether threatening place. New

parents study the reports of local street crime and global conflict which a brief time ago would have prompted a mere flick of the television remote to bring to attention pleasanter subjects; they find themselves reading the dark realities of human encounter with a sudden deep interest, involved in the minutest details in wholly new, personal ways, calculating the odds of "worst case scenarios" if the madness should reach their door.

The security-obsessiveness of the new parent brings into relief a phenomenon that is quasi-universal in homespaces of all sizes and politico-cultural-religious descriptions: the hypervigilance of those in roles of responsibility. We all share a common tendency, and all the more so when the homespace is young and untried against the destructive forces of the outer world, to double check the locks on the windows and doors, monitor the movements in the street, and keep a close eye on the neighbors and strangers who wander down our block.

But is security vigilance always that exaggerated? This question can only be answered phenomenologically—through an analysis of the lived experience of home and parenting, because the objective evidence of social science provides scant confirmation of the reasonableness of hypervigilance against strangers. But it matters not to the *human* experience what is the *actual* risk to the home and its inmates posed by external threat; what matters is whether the homespace is perceived from within as at risk from the outside. When people feel safe in their home settings, sheltered among their group, they concomitantly relax the rituals of security; they open their doors and windows a little, and regard the border stones and fences of their property simply as convenient meeting spots with neighbors and passers-by.

On the other hand, where homespaces sense themselves threatened, there exists the opposite tendency. Ingroup members, and especially those in control, often become obsessed by security concerns and begin to practice pathological rituals of defense. Doors will be bolted and windows secured. Differences passing by the portal will straightway signal danger and trigger alarms. Strangers and even neighbors will be interpreted as threatening and malevolent. Guards will need to be posted at every entrance to the dwelling. And inmates, too, will come under scrutiny and be held in close surveillance to ensure that they do not become seduced by the enemy to acts of treachery.

Psychologist Rollo May warns about the ethical dangers that plague those who take most seriously their responsibility toward others: "An extreme emphasis on individual responsibility can become an egocentric manipulation of others, a compulsion that defeats genuine morality."[1] This is to say, the most responsible masters of homespaces can pay a dual ethical price for their vigilance: they can become tyrants over their ingroup members, out of an exaggerated concern for their safety, and they can isolate the homespace and alienate it from the broader human world, becoming aggressive and threatening to their neighbors and to strangers passing by.

This dual-facing expression of hypervigilance to which the nodes of power fall prey in any homespace cannot help but remind us of Janus, the two-faced Roman god of the portal, whose split face was displayed above the massive gates of the great city of Rome. The god Janus has one aspect smiling, signaling welcome to friends; the other side of his face is snarling, menacing to potential enemies.

The Janus-face captures the dictum "Do good to friends and harm to enemies," one of the oldest and most respected rules of military and philosophical ethics. Its starkly dichotomous structure configures the training of the warrior class in all military societies since ancient Sparta. Plato applies this simple dichotomy as the logic that structures the training of the "watch-dog" guardian class in his second city of the *Republic*.

However, hypervigilance drives power nodes, in times of insecurity, to radicalize the oversimplistic dual-faced orientation of rigorous portal control. While the snarling face is still reserved for outsiders, it may be turned as well on those within who are perceived to present a threat. Periods of insecurity are often characterized by oppression and abuse of inmates, as well as toward external parties, while culpability for these extreme measures will be ascribed to outsider threats. The fact is that it is exceedingly difficult, in times of homespace insecurity, for those in charge of security to see their own violences *as violence*, rather than as acts of responsible leadership against (internal

---

1 Rollo May, *Power and Innocence* (New York: Norton & Co., 1972), p. 168.

and external) forces of chaos.

The leaders in the homespace, at their most responsible, then, may not be able to avoid twisting both sides of the Janus face into a menacing frown and reverting to an organizational structure that is oppressive to those in its care and aggressive to external parties. The impossibility of a leader's avoiding the temptation of internally and externally directed violences approaches its completeness the more he or she becomes obsessed with insecurity. In short, ingroup leaders become more aggressive toward ingroup members and more threatening to outsiders, the less they feel secure about their own leadership and/or their group's ability to withstand treachery or attack. Violence against perceived enemies begins with insecurity about the self. Fear and self-doubt drive hypervigilance, which fulfills itself in violent overflow on family, friends and enemies alike.

Nevertheless, the single most frequently used homespace ritual applied for securing the young is to arm them with "street smarts." We teach them to fear strangers and warn them not to converse with people from across the tracks. We counsel those we most treasure with the firmest advice: trust only those people whom you know, those with whom you have the most intimate connections. But the fact of the matter is that this counsel does nothing to prepare them against the violences that are most likely to confront them.

The research is extensive and unequivocal: people are at far greater risk of violent assault from intimates, the very people they count on for protection. The weaker members of the society, usually (but not always) women and children, are far more likely to be attacked, beaten, raped, knifed, and killed in their own homes or in the homes of trusted family members or friends, and at the hands of a protector or lover, than they are likely to be the victims of strangers. According to the U.S. Bureau of Justice Statistics, more than a thousand women are murdered by an intimate partner each year. Fifty percent of marriages experience one or more episodes of domestic violence; in twenty percent of marriages, the violence is ongoing. In the United States, a woman is battered by a loved one every ten seconds; three are killed every day. More than a third of the women treated for violent injuries in emergency rooms in the U.S. have been attacked by their husband or lover. According to the U.S. government's Bureau of Justice Statistics' "National Crime Victimization Survey," which includes unreported crimes as well as those reported to the police, almost 234 million women were raped or sexually assaulted in 2006, more than 600 women every day.[1]

Young, low-income women are the most vulnerable, and African American women are overrepresented in domestic violence rates; American native populations are victimized at a rate nearly double that of other races. But women are not the sole victims of intimate violence. Men report assaults at the hands of intimate partners in 2.9 million cases each year. In 2004, 1,544 deaths occurred from intimate abuse in the United States; 25% of these were males; 75% were females. Only one third of the cases of domestic violence fall into the classic male batterer syndrome. Equally common is the case where both men and women are active partners in mutual violent abuse. Women tend to abuse psychologically and verbally, and often the abuse is physical as well. But in cases where any real physical harm is done, the classic syndrome reigns supreme: men hurt women. Generally, diverse forms of harm coexist, perpetrated by both genders, despite physical harms offering the most obvious evidence.

On the other hand, women (and often those who are themselves abused) are more likely than men to harm children; women are perpetrators in 56% of the cases of child abuse in the United States. In 2007, 3.2 million reports to state and local child protective services showed 794,000 children to be victims of abuse or neglect: 59% of these children were victims of neglect, 4% were victims of emotional abuse, 8% victims of sexual abuse, and 11% victims of physical abuse. In that year, 1,760 children, newborn to age seventeen years, died from abuse or neglect. According to the Family Violence Prevention Fund, girls are at higher risk than boys for all types of child maltreatment, and children are at greater risk the younger they are.

So violence is well spread around in our modern societies. We could argue about whether, in the best cases of family organization in the Western world, men are more often the sole responsible power node. Certainly, decades ago, this was the over-

---

1   http://bjs.ojp.usdoj.gov/index.cfm?ty=dcdetail&iid=245   (retrieved November 14, 2012).

whelming social reality. But nowadays, it is far more likely that the role of familial leadership is role-distributed according to areas of perceived expertise, with women assuming leadership in some domains of family affairs and men taking over in other domains of responsibility. However, when it comes to questions of security, families, as higher-level sites of identity, have a tendency to revert to more conservative and authoritarian models of governance, when they feel insecure or threatened. Thus, the likelihood is that in times of chaos, men will step up as leaders to secure the fragile stability of the home.

Thus it is significant that the figures on violence against men are starkly different from those on violence against women. Men have a greater likelihood than women of being attacked by a stranger rather than by a friend or family member. So men, when they step into leadership roles, are rightly concerned about strangers and troublesome neighbors, whereas women would do well to beware of their partners, and children would be best warned to steer clear of their parents. Violence has a tendency to spread across gender and power status lines, but one thing is starkly clear: violence begets violence, and it is generally a deeply intimate affair. Men beat their partners; abused women neglect and harm their children; abused children hurt their younger siblings.

Thus arises the paradox of home. We most fear those outside the safe walls of the family home, when we are actually at greatest risk around those who love us and share our homespaces. The hypervigilant leader, whatever the gender, may safeguard the domicile with a suffocating responsibility that stifles freedom and growth among the wards. This reality is slower to reach the public domain because information flow can be more easily contained in the home than when obsessive security measures overflows on neighbors and strangers, where they may in turn trigger aggressive counter-responses. We teach our children to beware of strangers, when the evidence is clear: they are much more at risk in the security of their homes than they are in the company of strangers.

Despite the fact that human beings tend to think of themselves as highly rational creatures, and despite the overwhelming evidence that people are at greatest risk of harm in their own homes, social scientific research data has little purchase on people's lived sense of the world. What matters most is where and with whom people *feel* vulnerable or secure. On the most basic level of rationality, where fear tends to function best, we cling to those people who look most like us, dress as we do, talk as we do (and without an accent), and share our belief systems. When we feel threatened, we pull back to the familiar, and we see malice in the different.

Since hypervigilance is driven by the deep-seated passions ("affects") of fear and self-doubt, we may expect that people who act violently against others have ceased to be reason-able. However, reason is a powerful and useful faculty that can readily be conscripted to justify violence in the name of homespace security. Reasons will rush to defend violent acts against those who appear threatening. Sociologist Neil Smelser explains:

> It is one of the most profound aspects of evil that he who does the evil is typically convinced that evil is about to be done to him. He regards the world or at least a part of it as dangerous and bent on destruction and therefore something justifiably to be destroyed.[1]

A special cognitive framework is erected in the face of the alien. Through this framework, the merely "different" comes to be viewed as exaggerated in potency and malevolence—as "evil." A distorting cognitive framework can be shared across broad landscapes of identity by whole families, religious groups, ethnic groups, and entire states, when they feel confronted by a common enemy. The suspicion of the different can quickly burgeon into an all-embracing ideology and may even become institutionalized and passed on from generation to generation. In individuals and in human groups, distorting cognitive frameworks breed pathological responses that readily sanctify violences against alien others.

Moreover, the purgative violence that casts out the evil alien in turn sanctifies the brave warrior who was willing to take up the sword. Thus demonization and murder of the different

---

1 Neil Smelser. "Some Determinants of Destructive Behavior" in Sanford and Comstock, eds., *Sanctions For Evil.* (San Francisco: Jossey-Bass, 1971), pp. 15-24, p. 17.

comes to be assigned deep social and ethical significance in the homespace worldview, and when the dark deeds are done and the monsters purged, "myths of innocence" are spawned to sanitize the purgative violence and celebrate the acts of bravery.[1] Violence, repression, murder, and war become matters of glory and celebration, instead of human tragedies.

I have stated that hypermasculine, authoritarian and militaristic virtues are called upon during times of social chaos. But these are not the sole virtues of the homespace. The predominant virtues during happier, more secure times, when fear and self-doubt have slipped to the background, are associated with the welcoming aspect of the home and its gentler mission of nurturing the inmates and welcoming neighbors and hosting passers-by. Though these feminine virtues are entirely appropriate for dwelling in a world of infinite differences, they can nevertheless put the homespace at great risk.

The practice of virtues such as gentleness, generosity, and compassion can only ever be temporary and provisional, since by their very nature they throw the homespace into vulnerability, which it can hardly afford for great stretches of time. We can only feed the beggars so many meals before our pantries are bare and our own children hungry. We can only give beds to a limited number of waylaid travelers before our children are sleeping on the floor. And there is a worse danger to too much generosity: all these strangers bunking in our quarters and invading our larders can harden our hearts. We soon discover that taking on the responsibility to host the needy is never ending and often thankless, so the greatest risk of helping others is the moral one: we can become heartless and insensitive to suffering, when we see it every day and when it encroaches on our table and between our bed sheets.

Social scientists Viola Bernard, Perry Ottenberg, and Fritz Redl warn that face-to-face confrontation with a suffering world is dangerous to the onlooker's sense of compassion. In their article entitled "Dehumanization," these experts describe the desensitizing effects of witnessing extreme suffering. They

---

1 Neil Smelser states: "Myths of innocence enjoy a more or less universal and permanent existence [though they] tend to be activated only under certain historical conditions." (Ibid. p. 20).

tell that, in a surprisingly short duration of time, witnesses to atrocities become hardened to the sight of suffering and lose their ability to empathize with the afflicted.[1] Before long, report the scientists, the witnesses begin distancing themselves from the suffering, cognitively separating themselves from the victims with such defensive myths as "that could never happen to *me*; I am not like *those people*." The victims become less human in the eyes of their observers. Witnessing this phenomenon has led our scientists to the general conclusion that bystanders to affliction themselves become "less human," because they sacrifice the human capacity to feel empathy for their kind.

So a *bidirectional* emotional hardening turns caring witnesses into desensitized, apathetic robots, just as it turns suffering persons into robotic specters, such as the "musselman" phenomenon of the Nazi death camps. Emotional hardening is not only undesirable for its existential effects; it is dangerous. It makes people unpredictable and prone to aggressive overflow. Social scientists report that "the constructive self-protection [that dehumanization] achieves will cross the ever-shifting boundaries of adaptiveness and become destructive, to others as well as the self."[2]

Whether the homespace presents its menacing face to threaten enemies or its hospitable face to welcome outsiders, it seems rarely to feel completely "at home" in the world. It is ever placing itself in a state of moral or physical risk that can ultimately fulfill itself in aggression, no matter how generous and nurturing it sets out to be. Homespaces, by necessity, must find

---

1 Psychiatrist Robert J. Lifton, has written about the reactions of Hiroshima survivors to the mass deaths and devastation of the bombings. At first, Lifton reports, the witnesses were overcome by the utter horror of the carnage—the dreadful burns and disfigurements, the carcasses strewn about, torn in pieces and stripped of skin. Witness could find no words to express their initial reactions. However, in a remarkably short while, tells Lifton, a common reaction was reported. "Each described how, before long, the horror would almost disappear. One would see terrible sights of human beings in extreme agony and yet feel nothing." ("Psychological Effects of the Atomic Bomb in Hiroshima: The Theme of Death" in *Daedalus, Journal of the American Academy of the Arts and Sciences*. 1963. pp. 462-497, p. 92).

2 Viola Bernard, Perry Ottenberg, and Fritz Redl. "Dehumanization" in *Sanctions For Evil*. Nevitt Sanford and Craig Comstock, eds. (San Francisco: Jossey-Bass, 1971), pp. 102-124, p. 107.

ways to stabilize their territories and secure their borders. They must keep the inside safe and the outside out, if their identity is to make any sense. Only stable markers of identity can resist the ebb and flow of material decay and temporal corrosion, and secure the homespace against the death-bound forces that carry all entities into dissolution.

Homes must resist the passing-away aspect of their own coming-to-be. They must resist the internal tendencies toward pathological enclosure that suffocates indwellers and defeats the lived experience of the home as gentle, nurturing and hospitable. But they must also resist foolhardy generosity, if they are not to be consumed into the menacing chaos of the hungry world at large. Homes must simultaneously maintain their Janus faces, their conflicting yet necessary dual aspects, if they are to endure as viable sites for human dwelling. But managing the dual visages is no easy task: every view that the homespace has of the world, whether from the barred windows of the fortress-prison or from the wide-sprung portal of the welcoming refuge, the homespace is constantly at risk of reverting to violent pathologies.[1]

We can state therefore that the home has a paradoxical structure whose logic fluctuates along a continuum between two extreme and radically opposed states of being: xenophobic withdrawal into safe (if suffocating and cognitively distorting) interiority and foolhardy generosity to otherness. Periods of openness ultimately return the home to a logic of hyper-responsibility that fulfills itself in obsessive self-assertion and dehumanization of difference. In whatever mode the home is currently functioning—whether its self-protective warrior virtues are alert at their post or whether its feminine virtues throw open the doors in joyful acceptance of the world—the ultimate result is

---

1 Walter B. Cannon, in his celebrated work, *The Wisdom of the Body* (New York: Peter Smith Pub., 1978), tells that there are three possible reactions to situations of threat: flight, fight, or delayed response. We may attack in an immediate and cathartic explosion of violence, we may run away and hide, or we may bide our time for a more thoughtful, perhaps more subtle, violence in a future opportunity. Rollo May has argued instead that those who run away and hide *are* those who lie in wait, and he claims that this group is the most dangerous of all. What they await is sometimes a titanic explosion of destructiveness (*Power and Innocence*. New York: Norton & Co., 1972).

the same: a cognitive framework that attaches daemonic significance to wayward inmates as well as to neighbors and strangers. Whatever aspect of its mission the home is currently serving, it is likely to ultimately flare into destructive pathologies of defense, oppressing those within the structure and rebounding upon those beyond its doors.

The homespace is a highly ambiguous site, where phenomenologically much good is promised—and expected—for indwellers, but where much harm can be done, internally and externally, when the doors slam shut to secure and repress indwellers and when they are thrown wide open in carefree generosity. Undoubtedly, people need stable and secure homespaces where they can carve out their unique identities and find themselves in terms of their values, goals, and moral and spiritual lives. Since fear and self-doubt foster aggression, a strong and confident sense of self is the surest remedy against the negative emotions that undersit much of the aggression we witness in the world. However, our conscious minds and our lofty ideals are not always in control of our actions. As much as we possibly can, we must bring into the glaring spotlight of rational scrutiny the hidden forces that drive us subterraneously. We are like an enormous iceberg floating across the ocean, whose lofty tip believes itself to be the helm, consciously directing the iceberg's course, while in truth the course is being navigated by ancient and relentless forces deep below the surface—the inexorable weight of histories and the power of instinctive energies imbedded in the icy matter, hidden far below the captain's line of vision.

We shall discover in the following chapters the nature of those subterraneous forces and their continuing power to orient our behaviors. We will also see how current societal forms exert environmental pressures which nurture violent responses to the human situation. Homes are the sites where our hearts are most invested and thus where we may be more prone to impassioned hyper-responses to threat. This is why it is so important that people bring rigorous attention to the values that orient identity work, and challenge the goals that drive them headlong into allegiances of identity, which necessarily exclude others. When we consider the rituals that are called upon to establish ourselves as distinct from others, we will appreciate how the very forces that give us ingroup identity and a sense of belonging to others we value and love are the same dangerous forces that give us exclusion and violence, at the homespace and in the world at large.

CHAPTER FIVE. THE NATURE OF HOMESPACE VIOLENCE

Despite the prevalence of the language of "human nature" in popular and political discourse and despite millennia of effort by philosophers and more recently by psychologists and genetic biologists in carving out their various theories of "human nature," without the slightest degree of certainty can we attribute any notion of fundamental "nature" to the human species. Here the Buddhists have it right: all sentient beings are fluctuating realities, "dependently co-arising" according to causes and conditions. As useful as our categories and theories are in permitting a stable sense of identity, the disquieting truth is that there exists no stable "self" or "soul" and no essential characteristics that determine us as human or distinguish us from the sub- or non-human.

However, the truth or falsity of the idea of human nature is not what is at stake in this chapter. However logically impossible it may be to appoint stable characteristics—a "nature"—to fluctuating beings, human beings do share common histories and prehistories, that predispose them for certain attitudes and behaviors in certain conditions. Moreover, humans do share a common, if constantly fluctuating, gene pool, a pool that matches by almost 99% the gene pool of the chimpanzee and bonobo primate families.[1] The idea of human nature is fervently held by many scholars across many disciplines, as well as by many lay-persons. It is popular because it proves exceedingly functional, serving both good and bad ends. It is a useful metaphorical tool for speaking of common tendencies and dispositions that bind diverse members of the species into a common human family, but it is also useful for some groups in making claims of elite status among their kind, among whom they claim to compare favorably with others less human or subhuman.

The idea of an enduring self with a set of essential character-istics to be enhanced or vigilantly monitored can be a useful con-cept in virtue ethics, to measure an individual's moral progress, and to chart the evolution of the soul along a moral trajectory. But the same useful concept can be, and has been, badly mis-used to attribute differential value to different individuals and varied cultures, to attribute "normalcy" and "deviance" to some members within groups, and to posit superiority to some groups among others. Whoever has the political and epistemological clout to control the definition of normal "human" characteristics is in the advantageous position to posit himself and his kind at the summit of the evolutionary ladder, as prime specimens of the species. All discourses about human nature are pure fiction, but that does not stop them from being politically and socially func-tional wherever they can be sold as truth.

For an example of how the discourse of human nature serves certain groups or individuals and does disservice to others, con-sider any definition of human beings. Aristotle argues, for ex-ample, that human beings are "rational animals." If we accept this definition of our common human nature, we are faced with a troubling corollary: anyone who does not strike us as adequately rational, or rational in the same way that our culture applies rea-son, could logically be said to be less than human (subhuman) or so far below the standard of our common reason so as to slip from the scale altogether (nonhuman or inhuman).

We witness the concept of human nature hard at this ex-clusionary and dehumanizing work in the hands of Social Dar-

1 Mikkelsen, Tarjei, et al. "Initial sequence of the chimpanzee genome and comparison with the human genome." *Nature* 437.7055 (2005): 69-87.

winists as they constructed their hierarchical ladders of differing human cultures from evolved, rational, fully human beings (themselves, white European males) to less evolved subhumans (Africans and other indigenous peoples across the globe). The notion of human nature permitted the foreign invaders not only to make sense of the ethnic and religious differences they encountered in the human family, it provided them with the logical categories to construct their justifications for slaughtering and enslaving the "less human."

Thus it is with great trepidation and many disclaimers that I enter into the discourse of "human nature" in this chapter, as I review a spectrum of the theories of human nature that have been called upon to explain intraspecies violence. It is crucial that the reader maintain a diligent awareness that these are merely theories, and dangerous ones for the reasons cited above. In entertaining these theories for the purpose of considering what hidden forces may underlie our human behaviors, we should speak only in the vaguest terms of general predispositions and propensities, leaving plenty of room for human differences in the similarities that our theorists will posit.

For the most part, the philosophical debate about human nature has followed the two extreme deviations of moral attribution: "human nature as basically good" or "human nature as basically evil." An example of this debate within a single philosophical tradition is seen in the two great Confucian sages, Mencius (371 to 289 BCE) and Hsun Tzu (298 to 238 BCE). Mencius tells Hsun Tzu that human nature is akin to water; it has its natural ways of flowing.

> [W]ater does not show any preference for either east or west, but does it show the same indifference to high and low? Human nature is good just as water seeks low ground. There is no man who is not good; there is no water that does not flow downward. Now in the case of water, by splashing it one can make it shoot up higher than one's forehead, and by forcing it, one can make it stay on a hill. How can that be the nature of water? It is the circumstances being what they are. That man can be made bad shows that his nature is no different from

that of water in this respect.[1]

Mencius goes on to explain how good people go astray:

> In good years the young men are mostly lazy, while in bad years they are mostly violent. Heaven has not sent down men whose endowment differs so greatly. The difference is due to what ensnares their hearts . . . What is common to all hearts? Reason and rightness. . . . Benevolence is the heart of man and rightness his road. Sad it is indeed when a man gives up the right road.[2]

On the contrary, Hsun Tzu argues:

> Human nature is evil; goodness is the result of conscious activity. The nature of man is such that he is born with a love of profit. If he indulges this fondness, it will lead him into wrangling and strife, and all sense of courtesy and humility will disappear. He is born with feelings of envy and hate, and if he indulges these they will lead him into violence and crime and all sense of loyalty and good faith will disappear.[3]

How then do human beings overcome their evil nature and find the right path? Hsun Tzu explains:

> A warped piece of wood must wait until it has been laid against the straightening board, steamed and forced into shape before it can become straight; a piece of blunt metal must wait until it has been whetted on a grindstone before it can become sharp. Similarly, since a man's nature is evil, it must wait for the instructions of a teacher before it can become upright, and for the guidance of ritual principles before it can become orderly. If men have no teachers to instruct them, they will be inclined towards evil and not upright; and if they have no ritual principles to guide them, they will be perverse and violent and lack order.[4]

---

1 *Mencius*, D. C. Lau, trans. (New York: Penguin Classics, 1970), Section 2.
2 Ibid. Section 7, 11.
3 Ibid.
4 Ibid.

Hsun Tzu is opposed to Mencius' generous position and addresses it directly:

> Mencius states that man's nature is good but I say that this view is wrong. All men in the world, past and present, agree in defining goodness as that which is upright, reasonable, and orderly, and evil as that which is prejudiced, irresponsible and chaotic. This is the distinction between good and evil. Now suppose that man's nature was in fact intrinsically upright, reasonable, and orderly—then what need would there be for sage kings and ritual principles? The existence of sage kings and ritual principles could add nothing to the situation. But because man's nature is in fact evil, this is not so.[1]

Curiously, Mencius and Hsun Tzu begin from diametrically opposed positions regarding human nature. Yet they end in precisely the same place. They both attribute the determining force of human behavior to the peculiar conditions of the individual life—to nurture, not to nature. Where Mencius speaks of the "circumstances" that hold water uphill against its natural flow, so Hsun Tzu explains human evil with the impassioned observation: "Environment is the important thing! Environment is the important thing!"[2]

Ancient Greek philosophy approaches the question of human nature sympathetically, agreeing that "all men seek the good." Agreeing that the good is the shared human goal, the ancient philosophers assume their tasks of figuring out where people go wrong in their charting course for that lofty destination. In the allegory of the cave at *Republic* 588 to 591, Plato fashions the path to the Good as an uphill climb out of a cavernous city, where honors are distributed for learning well the messages propagandized by the unscrupulous leaders who control public opinion.

In this allegory, human beings are pictured as prisoners, fettered to the opinions of our leaders and incapable of breaking free of the falsehoods that frame our sense of reality. The prison-

1 Ibid.
2 Ibid.

ers must await the return of the philosopher who is standing in the meadows above the cave, gazing upon the sun-like Good, and reluctant to tear herself away, but for the pity she feels for the others still chained below in their ignorance. The cave allegory is a harsh critique of our earthly cities and shows how manipulable human nature is in its untrained, unphilosophical state.

The "Great Beast" of custom and popular opinion (*doxa*, as opposed to reason, *logos*) can have a devastating effect upon our course, diverting our nature from arriving at its destination, the good. We suffer a natural frailty of condition that inclines us toward excesses in appetite and passion. In the *Phaedrus* (246d & ff.), Plato specifies the quality that undermines our best efforts at harmonious community and challenges our individual ethical success. The name he gives to the troublesome quality is *phthonos*. *Phthonos* captures all the negative qualities that waylay human beings on the road to the good—greed, lust, jealousy, avarice, competitiveness. Plato states that this is the one feature that separates us from the choir of the orderly gods, causing us to battle, push and shove our companions on the steep ascent to moral perfection, rather than helping each other along the road to success.

Phthonos, as it is posited in the *Phaedrus*, seems to be an essential and universal aspect of human nature, a bad thing that gets in the way of our accomplishment of the good. This reading logically accords with Plato's description of justice as the definitive human virtue that renders both justice and our humanity not as something we already are, but as a moral goal to be achieved. We may be burdened with troublesome forces (*phthonos*) that cause us to harm one another, but by bringing the harmonizing influence of justice (*dikaiosune*) to bear upon our appetites (lust and greed) and our passions (anger and aggression), we can help each other up the steep slope to a balanced and harmonious life under reason's skillful jurisdiction.

Aristotle too holds that "all men seek the good," but he sees people going morally astray as a result of seeking ill-chosen goods. Their loves are out of whack. In the *Nichomachean Ethics*, Aristotle argues from the premise that the good life is the life that best fulfills the function for which the thing is designed.

Since the proper function of human beings is "an activity of soul which follows or implies a rational principle" (NE 1098a 6-7), then the reasonable life is the happy and good life. Beyond the "nutrition and growth," perception and reproduction that we share with all the animals, human beings distinguish themselves by the rational capacity that steers us toward the shared satisfactions of communal and political life.

For Aristotle, all people seek the good, and they seek it by gathering together in the polis and living reasonably under the laws. But people are also different from each other and their journey toward the good often veers off course because they confuse various objects of desire with the true good of the rational life. People get their goods mixed up. The more vulgar type of person "identif[ies] the good or happiness with pleasure" (NE 1095b 15-16) whereas the truly rational person knows that "the life of money-making is one undertaken under compulsions" (NE 1096a 5-6), so money cannot possibly be a true good.

The better life than the merely pleasure-driven life is the political life, where people strive after honors. "People of superior refinement and of active disposition identify happiness with honor" (NE 1095b 23-24), Aristotle explains. But this love too is ultimately flawed, because honors are granted at the whim of one's social peers, who are riddled with jealousy and competitiveness. Love of honor renders one's happiness as fragile and fleeting as public opinion. The best life, concludes Aristotle, is the contemplative life of the philosopher, whose happiness does not rely on external goods or people. The philosopher finds happiness in a direct pursuit of the knowledge of the good.

For both Plato and Aristotle, reining in the wayward appetites and passions is the task of a good education, and segregation with the best of human company is the most efficient means of speeding that task along. In Plato's ideal state, as in Aristotle's best democracy, the lowest classes, always seeking pleasures, are kept to their specific labors in the fields and discouraged from coming into the city and meeting in the marketplace (where they will covet goods they cannot afford) or joining the debates in the Areopagus (where they will be seduced by silver-tongued demagogues).

The best education is fitted to the social station of the individual. The best are taken aside from the appetite-maddened crowd to build habits of right conduct by acquaintance with the "right people" who set the best examples for others. Then subtle and oft-repeated practice (Plato says "music and gymnastics") nurtures nature in the direction of right impulses, so we may be ready to act with good conduct when the moral moment arrives. Both Plato and Aristotle prefer their ignorant masses busy in the fields; they see democracy as a most unfortunate political error, destined for tyranny. Aristotle puts the problem thus: democratic virtue (love of money and other pleasures) knows no limits, so liberty soon becomes license and collapses into licentiousness. In speaking of the problem of ill-fated desires let loose in the democratic constitution, Aristotle abandons the language of education's nurture and falls into the language of nature: "for where absolute freedom is allowed, there is nothing to restrain the evil which is inherent in every man (*Pol.* 1318b38–1319a1).

In the modern era, the rational principle that defines human nature breaks free of the troublesome body that got the ignorant masses in trouble in Aristotle's democracy. René Descartes declares the new definition of the human being: man [*sic*] is a "thinking thing." For the moderns as for the ancients, reason composes the essential nature of human beings, but where rational certainty was forbidden among the ancients, under the prohibition against *hybris*, certainty became guaranteed by Descartes' "Discourse on the method of rightly conducting the reason and seeking truth in the sciences."

The method for indubitable truth was to break the object down into its smallest pieces, to fully understand the parts. As nonsensical as the method clearly becomes once applied to a living organism, Descartes assures us that if we simply follow his method and investigate the integral parts of the thing, we can put the whole back together again and enjoy a full understanding. This is because material beings, for Descartes, are utterly mechanical entities, like robots or clocks. So on the model of the clock, understanding the whole of a thing is a matter of breaking it down to its cogs and wheels and witnessing how the parts come together to perform their function. To know the parts in their functions is to know the whole in its deepest nature.

However, when Thomas Hobbes comes to investigate the basic nature of the thinking thing, he finds much more than an inquiring mind. He finds a mass of competitive and aggressive impulses. Everybody is out to kill each other in a "war of all against all." Hobbes describes:

> The difference between man and man is not so considerable, as that one man can thereupon claim to himself any benefit, to which another may not pretend as well as he. [So] they become enemies [and] endeavor to destroy or subdue one another [by] force or wiles [until each] master the persons of all men he can, so long, till he see no other power great enough to endanger him.[1]

Human beings are as dogs, eating dogs to pursue their interests, and thus a "Leviathan" sovereign is needed to keep the cantankerous lot from killing each other off.

This all may sound pretty farfetched. We don't recognize ourselves and our neighbors in this bloodthirsty description of human nature. Yet this view of our kind enjoys great following in the modern world, because it is so entirely politically functional. As long as we can convince people that their neighbors are out to get them, we can justify the competitive race to prosperity that pits one person against another, one nation against the others, and the wealthy nations against the impoverished masses, in a pitiless competition for limited resources. The argument that one nation should invade another "pre-emptively," because it is looking suspiciously well-armed, rests entirely on a Hobbesian view of human nature.

In the early twentieth century, the debate over human nature took a psychological turn. American psychologists John B. Watson and later B. F. Skinner initiated the new approach of applying the methods of science to human affairs to discover a science or a "technology" of human behavior. The question of why people behave the way they do became eminently simple, following the ancient principle *post hoc, ergo propter hoc* (after this, therefore because of this). Behavior became a question of causes. When behavior is observed, we soon see that behavior tends

---

1 Thomas Hobbes, "Of the Natural Condition of Mankind as Concerning their Felicity and Misery" in *Leviathan* (Waukegan, IL: Fontana, 1962).

along the line of habit: last time, I behaved this way; so this time I behave the same way. Perhaps, argued the behaviorists, if we just describe what people actually do, we will be able to predict what they will do in the future.

Anthropologists describe customs, political scientists record political action, economists study how people buy and sell, spend and save, produce and consume. All of this investigative activity is undertaken because scholars trust the assumption that what people have done before, they will likely do again. In other words, behaviorists trust the presupposition that human nature's fundamental element is the tendency to repeat whatever behaviors have formerly been practiced.

At this point, ethologists enter the discussion, seeking out innate behavioral differences among the species. The discourse turns to "instincts" instilled over long periods to evolve into behavior propensities or dispositions. They looked to animal behaviors too for insights into human destructive behaviors. Enter Austrian biologist Konrad Lorenz, with his Nobel Prize-winning book, *On Aggression*, which seeks to identify the causes of human behavior by tracing common and discontinuous behaviors practiced across the spectrum of living beings.

Lorenz explains aggression:

> Aggression, far from being the diabolical, destructive principle that classical psychoanalysis makes it out to be, is really an essential part of the life-preserving organization of instincts. Though by accident it may function in the wrong way and cause destruction, the same is true of practically any functional part of any system.[1]

By mapping the behaviors of animals and demonstrating how aggression serves the species well, and how each species has developed over time and evolution effective strategies that ensure against the "accidents" of function that cause destruction, Lorenz speculates upon the evolution of the human world to discover where we may have gone wrong in the history of our evolving instincts. He explains:

---

1 Konrad Lorenz, *On Aggression*, Marjorie Kerr Wilson, trans. (New York: Harcourt, 1966), pp. 44-45.

> Aggression . . . is an instinct like any other and in natural conditions it helps just as much as any other to ensure the survival of the individual and the species. In man, whose own efforts have caused an over-rapid change in the conditions of his life, the aggressive impulse often has destructive results.[1]

The problem is that humans evolved so quickly from stooping, thick-craniumed grass-eaters to modern *Homo sapiens* that the latter rather suddenly (in terms of evolutionary time) found their fingers on the triggers of weapons of such enormous destructive potential as to threaten the continuance of their, and all forms of, life. The all too rapid development from fire to nuclear weaponry meant that humans missed an evolutionary step; they failed to develop the minimal natural inhibitors that would stop them from killing each other off. Lorenz states:

> In human evolution, no inhibitory mechanisms preventing sudden manslaughter were necessary because quick killing was impossible anyhow; the potential victim had plenty of opportunity to elicit the pity of the aggressor by submissive gestures and appeasing attitudes. No selection pressure arose in the prehistory of mankind to breed inhibitory mechanisms preventing the killing of conspecifics until, all of a sudden, the invention of artificial weapons upset the equilibrium of killing's potential and social inhibitions. When it did man's position was very nearly that of a dove, which by some unnatural trick of nature, has suddenly acquired the beak of a raven.[2]

We might be tempted to think it quite wondrous that we humans avoided killing each other off over the millennia since we gained control of fire, but this would be a speculation grounded in a misunderstanding of the nature of our species. Though Lorenz is rarely given credit for his very balanced treatment of human nature, he shows clearly that to understand our species as *merely* aggressive, rather than as possessing aggression as but one

---

1 Ibid., p. x.
2 Ibid., p. 233.

element in an elaborate network of impulses, would be a gross misunderstanding of the complexity of human nature. He underscores repeatedly that it is not the case that

> our human predecessor, even at a stage as yet devoid of moral responsibility, was a fiend incarnate; he was by no means poorer in social instincts and inhibitions than a chimpanzee, which, after all, is—his irascibility not withstanding—a social and friendly creature. . . . [M] oral responsibility and unwillingness to kill have indubitably increased, [but] the ease and emotional impunity of killing have increased at the same rate.[1]

Lorenz convincingly speculates that from the dawn of human time, a sense of responsibility toward fellow humans exercised a significant inhibiting force. "We are safe in assuming that the first killer fully realized the enormity of his deed" and that "there was no need for the information being slowly passed around that the horde loses dangerously in fighting potential if it slaughters too many of its members for the pot."[2] Humans, very early on in the evolution of the species, knew better than to reduce their numbers needlessly.

That raises the question whether the upswing in aggression over the centuries of mounting global population has not depleted that rational inhibitor. Jonathan Glover, in his *Humanity: A Moral History of the Twentieth Century*, argues precisely this discomfiting thesis.[3] Nowadays, open aggression hardly needs to be called upon to narrow the numbers of the human family, and life becomes ever cheaper as the global population explodes. The death of this or that one individual or the massacre or extermination by famine, thirst, or disease of whole groups of people hardly endangers the continuance of the species. The problem indeed is quite the opposite: there are so many of us in a world whose resources are so unfairly distributed that people—and especially children—slip away daily in what ought to be shocking numbers (tens of thousands), and barely anyone notices. As

1 Ibid., p. 234.
2 Ibid., p. 241-242.
3 Jonathan Glover, *Humanity: A Moral History of the Twentieth Century* (London: Yale University Press, 1999).

medical advances, superior diets, and monopolized water rights prolong life for the prosperous few, the argument is often made that some people rightly *have* to go, as though disease and hunger were nature's way of deciding who deserves to live. This is the message underpinning American ecologist Garrett Hardin's "Lifeboat Ethics," which suggests that there are too many people struggling to survive with limited planetary resources, and the choice facing those few who enjoy seats in the "lifeboat" of decent living standards is to paddle away from the hungry masses before the latter pull everyone under.[1] While it is true that population explodes primarily in the countries who can least afford to feed more hungry mouths, it is equally true that as societies improve their standards of living, population rates drop off, suggesting other, more humane cures for the problem of overpopulation.

Popular cynicism about the value of (some people's) lives is exacerbated by the ease with which killing can be accomplished at a comfortable distance from the killer, with modern long range weapons and unmanned killer "drones" that remove the risk factor (and the need to identify the enemy or answer to global conventions on war) from modern executions. Lorenz worried that we humans have too few inhibitors, but modern killing has rendered murder unreal, bloodless, neat and clean, from the distances we now effect it. We can push a button, drop a bomb, and kill great masses of people on the far side of the globe, beyond the range of the rulebooks and the claim of human emotions that, at closer range, would hold us back from destructive behaviors against our own kind.

The problem is not simply that we have aggressive urges but that people in the modern era do not enjoy an adequate number of healthy outlets for those aggressive urges. Hitler's Youth come to mind, as Lorenz explains that people, and especially youth, are prone to the syndrome of "militant enthusiasm," a readiness to abandon mundane concerns to follow "the call of what, in the moment of this specific emotion, seems to be a sacred duty."[2] This "phylogenetically programmed behavior mechanism" in-

---

1 Garrett Hardin. "The Tragedy of the Commons" in *Science* 162 (3859): pp. 1243–1248 (1968).
2 Lorenz. *On Aggression*, pp. 259-60.

teracts with culturally ritualized social norms and rites, and is highly prone to miscarry tragically.

> The ganging up on an individual diverging from the social norms characteristic of a group and the group's enthusiastic readiness to defend these social norms and rites are both good illustrations of the way in which culturally determined conditioned-stimulus situations release activities that are fundamentally instinctive.[1]

Militant enthusiasm has the predictability of a reflex, but through "intelligent and responsible supervision" this instinctive response can be conditioned to a new object, where it can be disarmed. Lorenz warns that localized social rites and norms are unfit objects for enthusiastic obsession, whereas humanity's greater goals (peace, eradicating poverty and hunger, child welfare, sustainable community) are worthy of enthusiastic support. However, anyone who has been to a peace rally and seen the protestors bashing their critics with their peace signs may be tempted to argue against the value of militant enthusiasm, even for promoting the best of causes.

Lorenz is a major voice in the discourse of "human nature." His work has fallen into disfavor in recent decades, as has the language of "instincts," which scholars claim admits of no firm definition. Furthermore, Lorenz falls victim to a criticism leveled generally against discourses about human nature: that their grounding assumption—that human nature is fundamentally aggressive—ends up providing support for aggression and war, since it affirms that the other guy is just as aggressive as we are, and is likely positioning himself for our murder, if we don't think faster than he.

Lorenz certainly finds aggression to be fundamental to human nature, older than the instincts to nurture and cooperate, which are born of aggression-redirecting rites. But the value of Lorenz's work on instincts cannot be overstated. His discussion of militant enthusiasm and the role of the sacred in destructive behaviors recognizes the enormous dangers associated with mindless adherence to local customs and rites.

---

1 Ibid., p. 251.

In the next chapter, we will turn our attention from nature to nurture, as we consider the origins of the sacred cultural rites and symbols Lorenz cites in his warnings against militant enthusiasm. We will see what the long history of those sacred ritual activities means for the nurturing destructive behaviors in the human family.

CHAPTER SIX. THE NURTURE OF HOMESPACE VIOLENCE

In the beginning was violence.
(Emmanuel Levinas[1])

Behavioral scientists, ethologists, anthropologists, hardcore Freudians, and philosophers of the Nietzschean tradition argue that "natural" forces or "instincts" are the determining forces that underlie conscious life and drive human behaviors. Human responses to environmental pressures, the argument runs, are structured in hidden biological recesses far deeper than the rational mind can fathom, by powers far older and more powerful than the fragile conscious mind can control or understand. Friedrich Nietzsche has his sagacious alter ego Zarathustra state in this regard:

> One thing is the thought, another thing is the deed, and another thing is the idea of the deed. The wheel of causality does not roll between them. . . . What is this man? A mass of diseases that reach out into the world through the spirit; there they want to get their prey.[2]

---

1 "The Temptation of Temptation" in Emmanuel Levinas. *Nine Talmudic Readings*. Annette Aronowicz, trans. (Bloomington: Indiana University Press, 1990), pp. 30-50. p. 37.
2 Friedrich Nietzsche, *Thus Spake Zarathustra*, Thomas Common, trans.

Like Nietzsche's "pale criminal" whose murderousness is being explained in this passage, we rarely understand aright why we do the things that we do. More frequently our explanations for our behavior arise *after the fact*. We are Epimetheus' students, though Prometheus, his brother and a seer, would be the better teacher. We go about rationally analyzing the sequences of actions that we have carried out, as though we can easily retrace our rational steps, as though those actions arose from rational deliberation, when in actuality, actions tumble out in chains of causation that have nothing to do with conscious intention. The best we can do is to invent reasons in retrospect for our deeds, fashioning our explanations to make sense of things that have their origin outside of the rational.

The task for the would-be interpreter of human behavior, then, is to discover the hidden forces that drive human beings to do the things that they do. They look to uncover the biological reasons for human actions, trying to locate "natural" forces that drive humans blindly, relentlessly, at the level of matter over mind. Ironically, the only way they can get at these forces, however, is to study human behaviors, looking for habits, repetitions, recurrent rituals of behavior that might offer evidence of these unseen pre-rational forces, evidence of instinctual life drives. Behaviors are identified and tracked, patterns are traced and plotted for frequency, and these patterns are then employed as interpretive devices to assert general trajectories of human behaviors. Then these patterns are reapplied to the future of human action. That is, looking backward to hypothesize about (pre)historic traditions, the biological determinist then looks forward to foretell what will be our species' fate; Epimetheus, the slow brother who only learns too late his mistakes, tries to teach Prometheus, the prophetic brother, the art of predicting the future, pointing his far-seeing brother's attention forward to speculate upon future possibilities for the species.

As a result of the concerted efforts of these backward-looking, forward-thinking scholars who study the logic of human behaviors, general agreement has been reached on a number of key themes about the (pre)history and the future of our spe-

(New York: Tudor, 1934), p. 35.

cies. Most crucial for our study of homespace violence are those anthropologists of culture who agree upon the theory that our species has practiced persistent behavioral traditions across the vast (pre)history of its existence. When behaviors are repeated over vast expanses of time, those behaviors tend to become more and more "ritualized" with each repetition. That is, reason falls away and behavior becomes more automatic, more routine, less mindful, and more habit-driven. Moreover, ritualized traditions in every society tend to become ever more rigorously controlled with respect to the time, place, and circumstances of their repetition, and the special identity of the people designated as the legitimate authority who are charged with overseeing the ritual repetitions. Furthermore, the ritual traditions become ever less open to dispute as to their fitness for current circumstances.

According to anthropologists, certain ritualized traditions have been practiced over lifetimes, over generations of lifetimes, over centuries, and even millennia. It is the work of these experts to disinter and track those traditions, speculate about their "meanings," and determine the social, political, and economic functions that those traditions served across the history of the species. Through understanding the traditions of the past, they trust that the lingering effects of ritual histories may be identified and brought from the gloomy depths of instinctual compulsion to the purifying light of conscious awareness, so people may be better prepared than our ancestors to distinguish those ritual traditions that remain adaptive and useful for species survival from those that have become maladaptive over time, forces embedded in our histories, our institutions, and our flesh that continue to have persistent influence over our behaviors as individuals and as groups, forces that drive us in future directions—for better or for worse.

The anthropologists tell a compelling story about a common ritual history shared across the diverse spectrum of geographical and cultural differences that characterize our species. On the one hand, those elaborate sequences of actions repeated over long periods of time with exacting attention to the details of their repetition have proven enormously helpful in getting human beings to the position of mastery of the planet that they enjoy today. Rituals organize the group and help them make sense of things. They grant solidarity and stable identity to the group and determine the patterns of relationship and interaction that structure the lives of the group and regulate its political and economic life. People repeat what proved useful in their past, and certain rituals proved highly functional in the early millennia of human time.

What is striking, however, is that those earliest rituals, which the anthropologists tell us were practiced quasi-universally by early human groups and across millennia, those very rituals that are crediting with propelling human evolution, were rituals of bloody murder sacrifice. Members of the ingroup were subjected to painful and terrifying experiences, and they were made to participate in murders and tortures of ingroup misfits and outgroup aliens. Pain and terror are highly effective pedagogical tools because the lessons learned through pain and fear are lodged deep within the psyche. There they configure the collective memory of the group, structure their common mental world, and provide their collective stories and histories. Rituals are bodily performances—performed by bodies upon bodies. Bodily practices come to settle deep into the resentment-riddled, guilt-prone, swaggering or timorous materiality of the culture's progeny.

When actions become ritualized, they are no longer simple actions, but rites with complex and ambiguous meanings, far beyond their ostensible social functions. When acts are repeated with crucial attention to the details of how they are performed (by whom, upon whom, at what time, in what place), they take on a portentous seriousness—a "sacred" import—in the minds of the practitioners. This is how traditions come to assume a "timeless validity" among the group, as representing eternal truths with benefits assumed to endure across the evolving circumstances of history. The practices that come to be obsessively regulated and practiced have profound import because they compose the markers of identity of the group. They mark the group as self-identical over the fluctuations of historical circumstances and distinguish them in clear and distinct ways from alien others.

All manner of valuable—and not so valuable—practices become sacred aspects of a people's heritage because every group needs these distinctions to find themselves as unique and valuable in a world of human difference. People become wedded to their customs, and they teach them to their children, not through intellectual analyses or rational arguments (which is why much of what we do makes little sense), but through long-repeated, unexplained acts and gestures and ceremonies—social rituals. People become bona fide members of their community by *doing what their people do*, so giving up what they do comes to be equated with giving up who they are. Change is experienced as treason, as a forsaking of the glory of the past, a treachery against the ancestors, and a betrayal of group destiny.

A group's ritual life, a vast web of powerfully conservative forces, composes the connecting thread of a people's history, the umbilical cord of group continuance, because rituals represent a prerational kind of communication, the most concrete kind. Rituals, as sequences of pragmatic actions and interactions rooted in an immemorial history, regulate all the crucial matters in the life (and death) of the group, matters of hygiene, sexual practice, marriage, and transition between the phases of life—birth, death, passage into adulthood, initiation into special functions within the fold. Rituals acquire a timeless validity, because they were originally adaptive, extending the life of the group across vastly fluctuating politico-economic circumstances.

Whether they remain adaptive or lose their efficaciousness under evolving historical circumstances, a group's rituals will still most likely be doggedly defended as utterly necessary, their necessity confirmed in the minds of adherents with each new repetition across each new generation. The very fact that they continue to be practiced will provide the proof that they must continue to be practiced; they will be perceived as empirically tested and proven against time. Ritual traditions thus have enormous emotional significance in the life of the group, though their origins and functions may have become utterly lost to group memory or, more likely, shrouded in myth. Nevertheless, the communicative power of ritual remains fully functional and powerful, even where they no longer have purchase in memory or understanding.[1] Many of the practices we observe today, from

1 See Walter Burkert. *Creation of the Sacred: Tracks of Biology in Early Religions* (Cambridge, Mass.: Harvard University Press, 1996), pp. 18-19.

marriage ceremonies to religious initiation rites to funeral arrangements, have their origins in rituals fashioned millennia ago by our earliest human ancestors.

Mircea Eliade has argued that myths comprise ontological and ideological disclosures that dictate visions of cosmic reality and patterns of dominance and exchange.[1] When we observe rituals in both their social and religious settings, rituals seem to go hand in hand with explanatory myths. For this reason, most people believe that rituals compose the performative articulations of myth. However, anthropologists are in solid agreement about the fact that rituals came first. Myths are a much more recent phenomenon than rituals. Myths are the symbolic articulations of deeper, older, *experiential* truths, prerational messages acted out in symbolic gestures, traditions, and ceremonies. Myths crop up *after the fact* to try to attach explanation to what previously defied explanation. As Nietzsche suspected, our thinking follows our actions, and not the other way around. Our explanations for what we do follow in the wake of our performances, our ideas and judgments configured by the prerational messages conveyed in ritual.

Actions, and especially ritualized actions repeated over vast expanses of time, speak to the core of our being. They seep into the very sinews of our bodies, permeate our feelings, and configure our desires, so that we find ourselves desperately "needing" to repeat the practices that have gone before. Actions become "imprinted" in our psyches and demand repetition precisely as they were learned. Walter Burkert, cultural and religious anthropologist, explains the biological process:

Biology has drawn attention to the phenomenon of "imprinting," an irreversible modification by experience, distinct from normal learning by trial and error; it is most notable in early stages of life. In fact, religious attitudes seem to be largely shaped by childhood experience and can hardly be changed by arguments; this points to the imprinting effects of ritual tradition.[2] The imprinting phenomenon explains why rituals have such an endur-

1 Mircea Eliade, *The Sacred and the Profane: The Nature of Religion.* Willard R. Trask, trans. (New York: Harcourt Brace Jovanovich, 1987).
2 Walter Burkert. "The Problem of Ritual Killing" in *Violent Origins*. pp. 147-176, p. 153

ing effect, in single individuals who practice rituals and in the collective memory and social imaginary of entire cultures. Imprinting also explains why rational arguments have insufficient emotional purchase to easily dislodge the pre-rational messages conveyed in ritual.

The case of violent and terrifying rituals deserves special consideration in this regard. Since the rituals practiced by early human communities were almost entirely centered around acts of bloody murder, excruciating tortures, and cruel expulsions from the community, their imprint was especially deep in individual and collective psyches. But since these types of rituals were imposed upon physical bodies, their imprint was also profound in terms of the genetic future of the group. After all, murders, castrations, and expulsions effect very real extinctions, exclusions, and ejections from the genetic pool of the group, so rituals had very real effects in terms of the genetic make-up of the group's progeny. Through rituals of this murderous and expulsive sort, the powerful individuals who oversaw the ritual life of the community (priests, kings, shaman, witches) not only controlled the religious and moral identity of the group; they self-selected for survival. They were in a position to fix and manipulate the biological composition of the group and to define, by elimination of the "contaminating" elements, the markers of identity peculiar to it.

For a number of reasons, then, ritual histories and their mythological expressions hold the keys to understanding human behavior today. Since rituals' core messages are prerational and subconscious, an understanding of homespace violence would be incomplete without addressing the rich palette of rituals that were practiced over millennia in the formative period of human prehistory. But ritual investigation is no comfortable objective study. We will discover truths about ourselves as we explore early hominoids. We can be certain that an exposure of the continuity between modern "identity work" and the bloody practices of human prehistory will challenge our reassuring assumptions of the moral progress of the species. On the other hand, perhaps illuminating this continuity will unsettle our sense of the sacredness of our homespaces, and force us to question the traditional practices that we undertake mindlessly, to be certain they are not consistent with the species' legacy of violence.

For studies of the ritual past of the human species, we must turn to the anthropologists who supply us with a rich bank of theoretical discourse on this intriguing subject. Their theories, qua theories, can only ever be speculative, since we cannot step back in time and test them for accuracy, and yet the number of consistencies across the various accounts, the degree of consensus about certain practices, offer us a fairly firm ground for studying our species' early ritual histories and speculating about their connections with our current traditions.

We have seen in the previous chapter that ethologist Konrad Lorenz understands human aggressive impulses, originally designed to ensure species survival, to have turned maladaptive early in the dawn of human time. Intraspecific aggression is an originally adaptive process. It helped in the early history of our species in the same way that it continues to help herd animals today: the rigorous "pecking order" established through intraspecific rivalry ensures that the hardiest and most aggressive individuals come to command the group both territorially and sexually, thus helping to maintain an even distribution of animals over a given inhabitable area and aiding in sexual selection for a healthier gene pool..

However, rituals of intraspecies rivalry turned maladaptive at the point where humans gained a relative freedom from environmental exigencies, beginning with the mastery of fire. In a famous passage, Lorenz tells:

> There is evidence that the first inventors of pebble tools, the African Australopithecines, promptly used their new weapon to kill not only game but fellow members of their species as well. Peking Man, the Prometheus who learned to preserve fire, used it to roast his brothers; beside the regular use of fire lie the mutilated and roasted bones of *Sinanthropos pekinensis* himself.[1]

Lorenz's diagnosis was so disturbing that it set off a great evolutionary debate during the 1960s, but by the 1970s, the idea of the instinctive *nature* of aggression was replaced by the idea

---

1 Lorenz. *On Aggression.* p. 239.

of the socio-biological *nurture* of aggression. At this point, ritual explanations for intraspecies violence gained prominence, as sociobiology emphasized the group over the individual consciousness. Groups as a whole could be ruthlessly self-interested and mercilessly competitive, and though groups are collections of individuals, experts began to focus upon the propensity for individuals to be shaped by the group to overcome any personal sense of responsibility or private conscience. So scholars began to recognize that the secrets to the worst human behaviors may be locked in the vault of social tradition, that sacred site where homespaces return generation after generation to initiate their young and affirm their solidarity.

The Ritual of the Hunt

Walter Burkert, classical philologist and anthropologist, in an impressive corpus (Homo Necans, Structure and History in Greek Mythology, Greek Tragedy and Sacrificial Ritual, The Creation of the Sacred, Ancient Mystery Cults and Greek Religion) investigates the problem of violence in human communities by combining historical and philological research with biological anthropology. The results are fascinating.

In his earliest works, Burkert assigns to the classical tradition profound importance for the intellectual and cultural development of the West. However, his investigations into classical rituals led him to the amazing discovery that the classical tradition was permeated with symbols and practices from much earlier epochs and different cultural traditions. Many of the Greek rituals of the highest period of classical culture, he discovered, were pre-Greek in origin and perhaps even prehistoric, though they continued to exercise an unwavering hold upon the Greek tradition long after the rituals made any cultural or religious sense.

The sacrifice ritual is one such pervasive anomaly. Long after its meaning had been lost, sacrifices continued to accompany festivals, mark the seats of oracles, and launch athletic games, the Greek theater, state ceremonies, and funeral observances. Cult gatherings and other mystery ceremonies continued to make ready use of sacrifice rituals. The uncanny endurance of these rituals led Burkert to an amazing insight: rituals require neither meaningfulness nor blind faith to remain operative and effective as rituals. Rituals remain ontologically and ideologically functional, even fully disconnected from their meanings.

Their functional endurance is probably attributable to the fact that ritual is prerational and preverbal, more primitive and ancient than speech, and logically (and ideologically) prior to stories, myths, and religious or philosophical arguments. Burkert explains the preverbal "messages" of ritual in terms of function.[1] To discover what kinds of functional messages are being communicated through early rituals, Burkert looks to the distant past of the species to the rich palette of ritual life in early hominoids. The earliest rituals, Burkert explains, centered about life's most significant functions—hunting, warfare, mating. The ways that groups approached their search for food, flight or flight practices under threat, aggressive displays to enemies or rivals, and sexual customs took on ritualized forms within the group, according to what was observed to work well and bring success to the group in feeding itself, protecting itself, and reproducing its offspring. Burkert argues that these ritual practices supplied a "common mental world" to the group. According to Burkert, many of the preverbal messages of these early rituals—their symbolic content, functional logic, and tone of seriousness—have been transmitted to modernity through an uninterrupted chain of tradition.[2]

Tradition consists of a conservative chain of condensed, systematized information. One of the most important functions of social ritual, explains Burkert, is to keep stable and finite the conceptual system of the participating community, against the fluctuating instability of historical changes. Ritual traditions employ a rigorous simplicity and a stark logic to serve this function. Strategies of inclusion and exclusion maintain clear and distinct analogies of reality, reducing the complex reality of the human drama to a core system of cultural "meanings" that hold sway against time. The simplest dichotomy of radically polarized meanings helps to orient those who would otherwise feel vulnerable and powerless *vis à vis* the infinite complexity and

1 Burkert. *Creation of the Sacred.* pp. 18-19.
2 Ibid. p. 22.

fluctuating realities of their environment.

The reduction of complexity, Burkert explains, rests upon a logic of two "containers"—good-bad, right-wrong, us-them, pure-impure, sacred-profane, friend-enemy. When new experiences or phenomena appear in the world and challenge reigning ideas, they can be easily sorted into one or the other of these two logical containers. From these sortings, then, hierarchies are constructed and links of causality forged, so that reality is reduced to the simplest schema of general concepts. Whatever fresh realities or experiences may arise, the simple logic of identity brings sense and meaning to them. The "common mental world" of social groups tends to adhere to this cognitively helpful pattern; a radically over-simplified, polarized worldview is the result of the quest for security and meaning in a troubling, fluctuating world.

In most communities, the belonging name themselves the "good" over against a threatening world of non-belonging, alien, menacing unknown. Often an "ultimate signifier" (god, chief, king, father) is added to offer easy solutions, where the simple polar logic cannot reach, so that the thorny human dilemmas that refuse to fit neatly into the two "containers," such as plague and war, can be left to infinite wisdom. Even the most oppressive domination, the most insecure conditions, the most unjust distribution of goods can be brought into moral equilibrium by the positing of a transcendent overseer to whom all must ultimately concede. Where resources are scarce and conditions of life deplorable, a transcendent gift system balances the cosmic ledger with promises of just desserts in a final accounting.

The sacrifice ritual's astounding endurance across the millennia of human time can be explained by the methods through which they are taught to the young. If we have learned anything from the wooden pointer-wielding nun of the old English convent schools, it is the learning force behind harsh forms of intimidation. Learning is most indelible where its memories are etched into consciousness through painful, humiliating, or anxiety-ridden practices.[1] Ancient ritual practices centered about animal and sometimes human sacrifices, painful purgatories, and excru-

---

1 Ibid. p. 29.

ciating physical mutilations. Children would be made to witness bloody mutilations, tortures, and murders firsthand. They
might be forced to handle the body parts, drench themselves in
flesh and blood, and sometimes drink the sacrificial blood. They
would be made to suffer and/or submit to whippings, beatings,
tortures, and murders. Terror and pain are certain to leave indelible scars that teach us profound messages about the human
condition.

However, it was not only the pain, terror, blood, and horror of the rituals that rendered the learning indelible. It was the
pain, terror, blood, and horror followed by culminating festivity. The sacrifice rituals always culminated in joyful celebration;
song, dance and laughter, with their repetitive rhythms and
sounds, gave vent to the pent-up psychic energies aroused by the
tortures and slayings. The rituals mimed the reality of life's ups
and downs and expressed the full sweep of human emotion, so
they could be experienced as the fullest and richest of collective
experiences. The chronology of the rituals etched into each suc-
cessive generation the cultural message that pain and suffering
are utterly necessary aspects of the human condition that give
rise to the fruits of community solidarity and joy. Everything
turns out fine in the end, as long as we follow traditions to the
letter: hence the remarkable endurance of murder rituals.

Once a tradition has been established in this spectacular and
affective form, the appeal to tradition is sufficient rationale for
its continuance. Burkert notes that much of Greek sacrificial
practice, for example the post-murder care and manipulation of
bones of the deceased, matches with reconstructions of Paleolithic hunting culture. Burkert therefore argues that the ritual
of the hunt provides a primal model to explain the origin of the
logic, acted out in the sacrifice ritual, that is, the simplistic, polarized logic that he identifies in the "two containers" theory, the
logic underpinning a culture's "common mental world."

The Paleolithic hunt is one of the earliest and most emotion-
ally-charged communal events and, being utterly crucial to the
survival of the clan, it was probably critical, contends Burkert,
to the creative construction of an orienting worldview for the

group.[1] Burkert argues that hunt rituals established and conveyed ontologies and ideologies that held the group organization tightly intact. During this early stage of human culture, when the only weapons were wooden clubs and spears hardened over fire, the intense collective energies of anxiety and terror, focused on the large carnivores, would have elevated the significance of the hunt far beyond the mere gathering of food. The ritual would need to rally the full range of survival strategies, restructure paradigms of aggressive behavior, and align the hunters, while reinforcing the patterns of ranking and ordering that organized them for cooperative focus. Intraspecific rivalries would be sublimated and rechanneled into political hierarchies and patterns of allegiances, to ensure the success of the hunt.

The hunt rituals, speculates Burkert, would have followed a simple structure. Pre-hunt ceremonies called forth the power of the ancestors to lure the animal into the territory. Then diverse ritual episodes (ceremonial dress, body paint, dance, role-playing) would funnel the anxieties evoked by the hunt into a common emotive channel. After the hunt, other rituals would allay the shock and guilt at the spilling of the blood of such a significant totem being. Later rituals added disclaimers of responsibility for the murder and establish the fiction that the powerful prey is a party to the success of the hunt, giving itself freely to the community by cooperating in his own murder. In this way, the hunt could be successfully inverted into festivity and the ambiguous energies of the participants could be purged. Culminating festivities thus celebrated the self-sacrificial animal, while the distribution of meats occasioned the primal moment of exchange upon which political and economic institutions came to be founded.

In Burkert's account, then, the urges of intraspecific aggression find release upon a new target, the prey. Over time, the simple hunt ritual propagates into more and more elaborate forms, until it gives rise to the full spectrum of social institutions and codes of conduct. Thus, Burkert states, "[t]wo sign systems, ritual and language, came to reinforce each other, to form the

---

1 For a comprehensive account of this theory, see Walter Burkert. *Homo Necans: An Anthropology of Ancient Greek Sacrificial Ritual and Myth.* Peter Bing, trans. (Berkeley: University of California Press, 1979), pp. 1-80.

mental structures that determine the categories and the rules of life."[1] The Paleolithic hunt ritual was so stabilizing that it not only outlasted the hunt, it endured for millennia in the form of the sacrifice ritual. It could be repeated any time that the social order fell into disarray. Burkert traces the hunt ritual into many later distinct ceremonial forms, including the archaic myth of the hero, classical Greek dramatic theater, and the European tradition of the royal hunt.

Like Lorenz, Burkert leaves us with a warning. He is convinced that the bloody origins of human community still remain fundamentally violent, hierarchical, and exclusionary. Burkert identifies the problematic legacy of ritual in the exaggerated seriousness and obsessive rigidity that characterize our collective responses to the human situation. Echoing Lorenz's concerns for human maladaptivity, Burkert asks: "What kind of a fitness is it that renders people unfit for change?"[2]

The Ritual of the Scapegoat Murder

René Girard, literary theorist and anthropologist of religion and culture, is one of the primary voices in violence theory. Girard has devoted much of his scholarly energy and expertise to unriddling the enigma of human intraspecies violence. His rich corpus presents one of the most important, if controversial, contributions to our understanding of how human communities have nurtured violence in their homespaces over vast stretches of time. In *Violence and the Sacred*, Girard opens with the stunning universalism that has come to characterize his work in general: he states unequivocally that violence is endemic to human society; it is the catalyst of human community. Violence has myriad forms but these polarize into two: the "good" violence of ritual (which, by definition, involves excessive regulation) and the "bad" violence that is its evil twin (because uncontrolled), best exemplified in the wars and pollutions that maintain for generations between families, tribes, or nations where there is no ritual outlet for their violent urges. Human beings must rely upon the "good" violence of ritual practices, primarily the sacrifice ritual,

---

1 Ibid. pp. 29-30.
2 René Girard. *Violence and the Sacred.* p. 300.

if they are to form communities and get along at all. Girard states: "Sacrifice is the most crucial and fundamental of the rites; it is also the most commonplace."[1] Girard is so impressed with the pervasiveness of the sacrificial ritual that he claims it as the *sole* unifying mechanism of the whole of human culture. He asserts:

> There is a unity that underlies not only all mytholo-gies and rituals but the whole of human culture, and this unity of unities depends on a single mechanism, continually functioning because perpetually misunder-stood—the mechanism that assumes the community's spontaneous and unanimous outburst of opposition to the surrogate victim.[2]

In the murder sacrifice, a victim is targeted for (more and less violent forms of) expulsion by a unanimous community. The solidarity purchased through this single unifying event under-lies, for Girard, all human creation, the institutional structures of human communities, and all the cultural and political arti-facts of the human world. Language, codes of etiquette, kinship systems, cultural prohibitions, marriage and procreation codes, all patterns of exchange and power, and all customs regulating birth and death, art, literature, and music—in short, all human endeavor—emanate from this single origin.

Girard argues that all this creativity began with an original "dark event," the collective ritual killing of a random victim. Thereafter, all creative endeavor comprises guilty and obses-sive re-enactments of the original event in order, to rearticulate the necessity and inevitability of the original event, in order to keep hidden its true randomness.[3] But it begs the question: why the original murder? This Girard attributes to another univer-sal phenomenon, a psychic mechanism pervasive to the human world, which he names "mimetic desire."[4] This mechanism rests

1 Ibid. p. 300.
2 Ibid. pp. 299-300.
3 Ibid. pp. 240-243.
4 Girard's theory of mimetic desire draws from Freud's theory of the Oedipus complex. Freud was the first to see conflict as the determin-ing socializing mechanism. But there are also irreconcilable differences between the two theories. In Girard, Freud's "father" can be any model or rival, while Freud's "mother" can be any desired object. Freud's "un-conscious" becomes, in Girard, the "mythic mentality." Ibid. pp. 201 ff.

upon the Freudian theory of familial rivalry that asserts: *I desire my mother only because my father, whom I value, desires her.* Violence is endemic because as one approaches more closely to the object of desire, he arouses the animosity of the one he truly values, the model (father). Thus arises the paradox of the veneration and rejection of the father figure, Girard's "double bind." In this paradoxical relation, the model remains venerated exemplar but at the same time becomes a "monstrous double" of the emulated model.

In Girard's theory, mimetic rivalry leads invariably to violence and one violent act spirals into cycles of violence until conflict fulfills itself in murder. One murder leads to cycles of reciprocal killings in an unending series of revenge murders, for so long as the killings continue to hold the same retaliatory meaning for both groups. The only way to end the cycles of violence, asserts Girard, is if both sides of the conflict can get together long enough to agree upon a scapegoat, attributed to be the real cause of the historical violence. The final killing of that random victim allows guilt for all previous violence to be purged from both groups at one fell swoop.

The murder is arbitrary and spontaneous, targeting a stranger without allies to champion his innocence or avenge his murder. He will always be a recognizable surrogate, however, who makes a believable "real culprit" for "just" punishment. All that is needed for the deed to be successful as a communal cohesive act is for there to be unanimous agreement about his guilt. Then a peculiar series of cognitive articulations follows: the victim will be treated as a criminal, denounced publicly, insulted, humiliated, beaten and whipped, and finally murdered (or symbolically murdered through beating to unconsciousness or expulsion from the community). The murder has a finality that halts the cycles of violence, and because the community can witness how much better things suddenly are, the justness of the murder is confirmed in their renewed communal integrity.

Without the final murder, Girard argues, the violence in the community would reach endemic proportions in the form of a "sacrificial crisis," the worst form of the "bad" violence that operates outside the control of reason.[1] In this crisis, cycles of reciprocal violence wear away the differences that separate the warring parties. No doubt they all begin to look like killers. Girard states that when identities lose their meanings, enemies cannot be separated from friends. Then, not even the blood spilt in ritual can be distinguished from the general communal murders. This is a crisis because societies are nothing but regulated systems of identities and distinctions. Where rituals of violence cease to regulate the rivalries and keep the identities of the rivals distinct, conceptual "order" collapses, meanings are lost, and the social structure topples.

Thus a horrible crisis is averted where the "good" violence of ritual expels ingroup murderous rivalries onto a surrogate victim. The only risk remaining then is that the victim will be recognized as innocent and the fiction of the "justice" of the murder will be revealed as fiction. To acknowledge the murder as the "dark deed" that it is, to admit the randomness of the victim, would be to plunge the community back into the spiraling horror. Therefore, in the aftermath of the murder, all memory of rivalry and rejection must be erased, while the beneficial consequences of the murder must be retained, to ensure closure of the spiraling violences. This is the task of religion, according to Girard's theory.

One cannot miss the Christian subtext, as Girard explains how religious ritual transforms the surrogate victim (Jesus Christ) into a collaborating participant in his own murder, collapsing the evil "monstrous double" into a self-sacrificing savior. The victim, demonized and murdered, is now exalted and divinized, and the beneficial effects of the murder, the renewed peace and unity within the community of murderers, become visible proofs of the blessings of the god on a guilty and undeserving humanity.

Girard finds it highly significant that the general loathing and disgust for the victim that precedes the murder (expressed in insults, curses, and beatings) is replaced, by the end of the ritual, by articulations of gratitude, veneration and worship. This polarity leads Girard to conclude that ritual effects sym-

---

1 Ibid. p. 46.

bolic transformation, monster into savior, ritual into myth, and communal atrocity into sacred religious rite. This "creative confusion" is so powerful a force, claims Girard, that it becomes the source of all forms of cultural artifacts—linguistic, conceptual and symbolic; social, political and economic.

Girard's tightly woven theory of the origin of the human world is unapologetically universalizing. Girard justifies this approach with the observation that the physiology of violence varies little across the human landscape, in methodology or effects.[1] Certainly this is arguable. Violence seems constantly to take on new and creative forms, continually evolving into new ways to humiliate and torture its victims. Responses to feeling violated are equally diverse, perhaps unique in every individual case. Girard has contributed much to the contemporary debate on ritual's effects but his sweeping generalizations have been a decided obstacle to his theory's general acceptance by the scholarly community.

However, what is most disturbing about Girard's theory is that the problem of violence and the measures called upon to resolve that problem are essentially the same. Girard's theory is scandalous because it rallies the logic of polar opposition to "order" the world's violences into those of which he approves and those he denounces. Rather than exposing the inadequacy of simplistic moral definitions, Girard reasserts ritual's logic in declaring some "good" and others "bad." Instead of collapsing the "religious worldview" that legitimates violence against the nonbelonging, he revives religious symbolism, especially Christian, as a still-effective tool to disguise the murderousness of human worlds.[2]

Religions remain integrally entangled in the problem of violence in human communities. With their obsessive rules and regulations, their excessive seriousness, and their polarized over-simplified worldview, they can readily be called upon to maintain the dangerous fiction that violence is "good" if enacted by the legitimate authorities. Girard does not challenge religion

---

1 Ibid. p. 47.
2 R. Girard. *Things Hidden Since the Foundation of the World*. Steven Bann, Michael Metteer, trans. (Stanford, CA.: Stanford University Press, 1987).

for their part in the general human destructiveness, of which they have done more than their fair share. Instead he celebrates the religious mechanisms that mask violence *as a problem* and that mask religion as in collusion with violence. In short, Girard's explanations of the origin of violence reaffirms the ritual ontologies, the over-simplistic, polarized understandings of the human world that promote the facile moralizations that trigger pathological responses, during times of unrest.

The Ritual of Rebounding Violence

Far beyond what our previous experts have reckoned, anthropologist Maurice Bloch emphasizes ritual as an enormously powerful force of stability in a community. Bloch's major works, *From Blessing to Violence* and *Prey into Hunter*, affirm the remarkable capacity of ritual to persist unaltered, even where radical upheavals in belief systems or in politico-economic circumstances have utterly uprooted and displaced people's lives. Bloch attributes ritual's power to endure and stabilize to its "logical infrastructure." While ritual is never isolated from the socio-politico-economic world, it is the one feature of that world that can maintain intact even where these environing circumstances are suffering radical upheavals.

Ritual, explains Bloch, has a minimal logical "core" that holds fast beneath the fluctuations of evolving historical socio-politico-economic forms that a society undergoes. But, more broadly, this logical core is, for Bloch, "quasi-universal" across the spectrum of ritual and religious practices, constituting "a permanent framework which transcends the natural transformative process of birth, growth, reproduction, ageing and death."[1] One might say that the core articulates the broader picture, standing back from history's troubling flux. The core message of ritual is a *pattern* of fluctuation that promises all crises will come alright in the end, if we simply ride the waves of violent turbulence.

Bloch demonstrates, through thorough analyses of a broad range of cultural groups, past and present, that rituals dramatize alternating episodes of social chaos and violent retribution.

---

1 Maurice Bloch. *Prey into Hunter: The Politics of Religious Experience* (Cambridge: Cambridge University Press, 1992), p. 3.

Ritual's core message is that history composes a dialectic of polar episodes of domination and repression. Life's energies flow up and down, blood and pain and terror sealing together diverse eras, powerful and powerless individuals, dead ancestral spirit and live tribal member, animal and human life forms, men and women, and old and young. The violent episodes that comprise the rituals evidence the episodic nature of the universe and the dual aspects of things, but they also affirm the necessity and efficacy of violence for unifying the diverse realms of existence. Violence seals human communities, manifesting the boundless power of the eternal, supermundane realm in the everyday. Rituals, therefore, communicate to participants that violence is necessary, valuable, rejuvenating, purifying, and restorative.

The rigid patterning of the alternating episodes of ritual acts out and informs the life patterns of the social group. Bloch maps out the patterning in his fascinating account of the circumcision ritual of the Merina tribe of Madagascar. The ritual opens with some incident of disorder, an indignity or violent offence perpetrated by one segment of the society upon another. The violation may be simply an act of minor theft from a group member or neighbor, or it may entail more serious offence, such as the seizure and humiliation, or even torture, of fellow tribe members or outsiders. The initial violence is followed by a reactionary violence, where the victims turn upon their attackers, humiliating and beating them in turn. The violent sequences move back and forth, mounting to a frenzy until someone (or some group) becomes marked off as "unassimilable." Once the group has targeted the victim, the ritual reaches its climax in the murder of the unassimilable one(s). The murder may be real or metaphorical. For example, in the rite of passage, a physical mutilation (circumcision) can enact the youth's "death" of consciousness and his/her "rebirth" as an adult member of the tribe. Or the violence may comprise an actual expulsion from the tribe of one of its less typical, less "belonging" members. Bloch insists on one dark fact, however: the occasional real murder must be carried through to maintain the seriousness of the event.

A common feature of ritual that Bloch notes is that the society's subordinates (women and children) always seem to be made to assume the early role of dominance in the ritual, beating or humiliating their social superiors. This stage, like the Greek festival when slaves and wives could temporarily disobey or mistreat their masters and husbands, enacts the breakdown of the social unit, dramatizing the chaos that ensues when the "rightful form" of the society is abandoned. Thereafter, when violence spirals in retaliatory cycles toward a final bloody climax—a murder or brutal mutilation—the chaos suddenly halts and everyone returns to the normal power relations. The core message of the ritual is clear: violence delivers order. Once the subordinate are returned to their rightful place (on the bottom of the social heap), everyone joins in a closing festival. The dancing, singing, drunkenness, and distribution of meats communicate to all that happy endings are guaranteed for the tribe when people take their rightful places in the social order.

Bloch calls the core message of social ritual "a logic of domination." But it is not a simple logic of "might is right." Rather, rituals are highly conservative because they assert, through their reciprocal exchanges, a fictional fluidity to the power structure. They allow the group to explore what life would be like if power were invested elsewhere than it is. The rite communicates the illusory "truth" that everyone in the social group has an opportunity to rule, but peace only reigns when the less fit to rule are returned to their inferior positions. Thus, by participating in the ritual, the oppressed members of the society actively and willingly participate in the enactment of the necessity of their own oppression. Ultimately, they can bear their humiliation with pride because they are participating members of a powerful social order that is powerful precisely because it is "rightly" ordered. Their willing submission to the social order preserves the strength, stability, and longevity of the tribe against outgroups.

Social ritual, then, for Bloch, function in every society—"quasi-universally"—to mask the reality of the pure exploitation of subgroups in every social order. Social orders only maintain stability and peace because women allow themselves to be exploited by men, children submit to parents, young defer to elders; upon this ranking and ordering violence, the social order rests. What ritual enacts, while it simultaneously hides, is that peace is a function of violence.

Only with the adoption of the ritual at the state level, as war against neighboring tribes, does the full ideological significance of the ritual come into view. When states overflow their violence onto neighbors, who are innocent bystanders of equal power to the aggressors rather than initiators of a first wave of ritual violence, the sheer gratuitousness of the violence is exposed. There is no collusion between inferiors and superiors, here, no willing submission of an "unassimilable." There is simply a powerful, aggressive society that, once internal order has been achieved, turns outward to dominate and conquer its neighbors.

Ritual's profoundly symbolic nature makes it a powerful medium for transmitting ontological paradigms and political ideologies. Bloch tells that "ritual does its ideological job and carries at its core a simple and general message which can be received and used [to effect and justify] almost any type of domination.[1] Ritual's primary message is that powerful societies exist because of the willing submission of inferiors within the social hierarchy. Internal violences are communicated to be necessary and desirable because they ensure the group's survival in the external world. This claim may not bear rational criticism, but since it is articulated *performatively* "in a hazy, non-discursive world, isolated from events and argument," it does not arise as a matter for rational inquiry.[2] Ritual performs the ideological work of affirming the rightness of the prevailing power relations, while relieving the powerful of the need to offer arguments defending their legitimacy.

The logic of domination is consistent throughout the entire structure, but it is most clearly evidenced, argues Bloch, at the political level in the group's foreign policy. In his *Prey into Hunter*, Bloch demonstrates the logic at work inside and outside the structure. The structural "core" of ritual, its violent energies ebbing and flowing, communicates that dual realms of reality exist—a weaker, mundane world that ever seeks to increase its power and status, and the supermundane world that feeds the vitality of the weaker realm when a connection can be forged. Ritual enacts the interplay between the two realms, the spiraling violence evidencing the increasing vitality which accompa-

---

1 Maurice Bloch. *From Blessing to Violence* (Cambridge: Cambridge University Press, 1986), p. 195.
2 Ibid.

nies that interplay. But since the phases of violence and counter-violence end in feast and festivities for all, the ritual evidences that grace arrives through the efficacy of "rebounding violence."

Moreover, during the final festival, the energies that have spiraled to a peak may be resolved in dance, drink, and feast. But often ritual violences do not simply find a peaceful resolution in communal feast, but carry over to the external world, in taunting gestures aimed at surrounding villages. Stones may be thrown, curses and insults may be flung, or the boundary markers may be removed and destroyed, signaling disrespect for neighbors and borders. These threatening climaxes to communal rituals expand the logic of the ritual beyond the "logic of domination" that keeps internal subgroups in submission toward an "idiom of conquest" (or "idiom of consumption") that displays tribal potency and extends the grace purchased through supermundane connection in the direction of extra-territorialization. Contra Girard, Bloch sees ritual violence of a single kind, a spiraling power demonstration, which has a strong tendency to overflow its bounds. Contra Girard's distinction between the good violence of religious ritual and "bad" unregulated (i.e., un-ritualized) violence, Bloch emphasizes the propensity of all ritual toward violent excesses due to their ontological and ideological underpinnings, their core of "religious" truth. For Bloch, religion is triumphalist and promotes violent extra-territoriality. Bloch states: "religion so easily furnishes an idiom of expansionist violence to people in a whole range of societies, an idiom which, under certain circumstances, becomes a legitimation for actual violence.[1]

To demonstrate how the "idiom of conquest" is effected, *Prey into Hunter* examines the initiation ritual of the Orokaiva tribe of Papua, New Guinea, commonly called the "pig people" for their practices of maintaining a familial relationship with that animal species, the pig. The Orokaiva raise their pigs much as they raise their children, suckling them alongside their human babies and lodging them just beneath the family dwelling. Throughout their youth, the young piglets romp and play with their human sisters and brothers. Then arrives the day when the human children

---

1 Ibid. p. 6.

will be initiated into the tribe in a complicated rite of passage. Much as in the Merina ritual, the early stages of the ritual are alternating episodes of rebounding violence, as the children of the village are chased about, beaten and terrified by an "outside group" (masked tribesmen representing the dead ancestors of the tribe). This episode of the drama enacts the hunting of the children "like pigs" to the chanting of "Bite, bite, bite!" They are chased onto the very platform where animals are ritually slaughtered at festivals. There, on the blood-stained podium, they are rounded up like animals by the strange intruders and then they are herded off to the woods. Terrified, the children submit to their attackers, while their parents, screaming and wailing at their children's plight, nevertheless deliver over their young to the spirit strangers.

Bloch calls this first episode in the ritual a "drama of penetration" (or "conquest" or "consumption"). Then, in the second episode in the woods, the boys are symbolically murdered; that is, they are locked in darkened huts, deprived of sight and sound, as though in a "dead" state. The dead children are fed strange magical foods, given new "voices" (taught to play the sacred flutes and bull-roarers that represent the "voices" of spirits), and taught new forms of movement, powerful spirit dances. After a considerable time of seclusion assuming their new identities, the youths are returned to the village. But the frightened prey who had been stolen from the village do not return as lost children to their parents, but they return as powerful hunters. Having survived their "death" and overcome the malice of the ancestors and the gods, the children are "reborn" as powerful adult members of the tribe—elevated, transformed beyond the mere human, purified by terror and pain, sanctified by contact with the transcendent, eternal realm.

Immediately upon re-entry to the village, the powerful hunters demonstrate their new newfound skills and potency by throwing themselves in pursuit of the pig-children, the animal brothers and sisters amongst whom they were suckled and raised. The hunters-become-warriors perform a triumphant warrior dance, sing the magical spirit-songs, and then, in a frenzy of newfound power, turn upon their helpless pig-siblings and slaughter the lot. There is much wailing and mourning at this cruel violence, which Bloch assures us is entirely genuine, for the mothers as much as for the hunters. For the latter, the slaughter is paradoxically "both a glorious fulfillment of their destiny and a moment of real sadness."[1]

The pig slaughter episode is followed by the usual festivities—the songs of triumph, the frenzied dances, the distribution of meats. But, as with the Merina, the violence does not end here. The ritual culminates in gestures of communal aggression toward neighboring peoples. In this closing drama, the entire village joins the new young hunters in acts of aggression against outsiders, removing the boundary stones surrounding the village, volleying provocative insults, threats, and curses at the external world. These gestures of tribal fierceness and hostility symbolize the renewed vigor brought to the tribe by the warriors' reconnecting with the spirits and the ancestors. But that aggressiveness is not merely symbolic and metaphorical. It is meant as an open-ended challenge to outsiders. Often the aggressive gestures generate real hostilities with outgroups.

Bloch demonstrates the pervasiveness of the core ontological and ideological structures of ritual and their tendency to seek violent overflow onto neighboring others by applying his theory to a broad range of diverse cultural contexts: ancient Greek ritual practices, biblical sacrifice stories, and current traditions of the Dinkas of the Sudan and the Buid of Mindoro. In each case, Bloch locates resonances of the consumptive/conquest idiom and the "logic of domination," and he points out their function as ideological links between religious belief and political/military aggressiveness. Bloch demonstrates in each case how the spiraling violences of the group's ritual practices express the escalating power (believed) transferred from a permanent transcendent realm to the mundane world. The rebounding violences, in every case, affirm the rightness of the rigid social structuring, confirm the necessity of oppression to the strength and power of the entire group, and fulfill themselves in aggressions toward external peoples.

Bloch's theory of ritual emphasizes, as does Girard's, the necessity of marginal beings or outsiders as sacrificial objects

---

1 Ibid. p. 12.

that permit purging of the aggressive energies and rejuvenation and solidarity among the belonging. As Burkert, Bloch shows that the festival distribution of meats is decisive in determining the distribution of power relations, the formation of political alliances, and the networks of exchange within the societies. Bloch's unique contribution to the anthropological discourse on ritual violence is the remarkable discovery that sometimes rituals compress and convey ideologies that are not merely absorbed into the subconscious of participants, but may be fully understood, knowingly executed, and willingly participated in.

Human rituals of intraspecific rivalry, rites of passage, and murder sacrifice or "scapegoating" rituals are just a few examples of highly conservative rituals that, according to most of our anthropologists, outlast their adaptive benefits, ultimately becoming "exaggerated to the point of the grotesque and the inexpedient," though Girard is the single voice in the anthropological crowd assembled here who argues for the adaptiveness of scapegoating murder rituals, naming them examples of "good violence."[1]

Lorenz and Burkert distinguish between rituals transmitted by cultural tradition across generations of practicing communities ("imprinting") and those passed on by way of selection or genetic heredity. This seems an important distinction, since it marks the border between the "nature" of human predispositions toward violent behaviors and the "nurture" of violent practices by continuing ritual within our homespaces. The latter holds out the hope that if we simply recognize a ritual as dangerous and discontinue its use, we can solve the problem of intraspecies violence. However, the distinction between nature and nurture is not as clear cut and meaningful as we would wish. Rituals that begin as social practices, such as the redirected aggression ritual (a ritual that whereby aggression toward a mate or other intimate is diverted toward a more remote, non-kin, or defenseless object), become "selected for" by our genes. That is, nurture practices, after long use, become part of our nature, subsumed into what Lorenz calls "the fixed instinct inventory" of predispositions favored by the selective process.[2]

---

1 Lorenz. *On Agression.* p. 42, c.f. p. 40.
2 Ibid. pp. 170-71.

Rituals, once they take hold in a society's traditions, one way or another alter the nature of that society, whether consciously accepted, enforced, and transmitted to the young, or silently absorbed into the gene pool. This claim approaches dangerously near the abyss of a "biological fatalism" that predestines our species to endless effects from the harsh practices of human histories. But this is definitively not the case. While human "nature" may disposes us in the direction of certain behaviors, these propensities are multivalent and contradictory. We may as easily cooperate, nurture, and negotiate with different others as strive to wipe them out. In times of peace and plenty, our inclinations toward the former tend to reign; in times of insecurity, when resources become scarce, conflict threatens, or natural tragedy strikes, our tendencies shift toward the latter, as we cling to those most like us and reject alien outsiders.

Lorenz was no biological fatalist. He is very clear in his assertions that humans can, over time, alter even the most fundamental aspects of our "instinct inventory." However, changing who we are by nature would require a profound commitment to healthy nurturance practices. In the final analysis of the situation facing the human species, Lorenz is not overly optimistic. He closes *On Aggression* with the indictment: "how abjectly stupid and undesirable the historical mass behavior of humanity actually is."[1] Altering maladaptive behaviors is no easy task but if we fail in this task, we will never alter our gene pool and escape Lorenz's stark prediction—that we will be doomed to the biologically just deserts of species extinction.

We cannot know with any certainty how much of this early common history of ritual violence remains lodged deep down in the nature of modern human beings. But if Jonathon Glover is correct, the last century alone proves time has not morally enhanced our kind. In *Humanity: A Moral History of the Twentieth Century*, Glover traces what he deems a "moral slide" from evil deed to more evil. It seems that modern human beings have learned well the lessons of a long history of violence and while they may be reluctant to take the next step toward cruelty and carnage, a step taken is difficult to turn back, and so the species descends

---

1 Ibid. p. 237.

ever lower into the hell realms of interspecies violence. Once we got the stomach during World War I for starving out women and children to win the war, it was only a small step farther to drop incendiary bombs on heavily populated areas, such as Dresden, to win the Second World War. Glover draws a straight logical line downhill from the First World War through Hiroshima to the American atrocities at My Lai. We may now add the most recent chapters to the moral slide Glover posits: the Abu Ghraib prison tortures, a vast global network of torture inside secret CIA prisons, and the use of killer drones to murder untried suspects on the far side of the globe.[1]

How violent are human beings *by nature*? Perhaps Richard Wrangham and Martin Muller put it most clearly: "biological determinism is misconceived. All the authors in [our] book share the biologists' conventional view that because phenotypes depend on interactions between genes and environments, individuals' behavioral strategies are not predictable from their genes alone."[2] However, Muller and Wrangham rightly conclude: of the primate cousins to whom we are closest in genetic make-up, the bonobos and the chimpanzees, human beings are definitely closer to their chimpanzee cousins in the high level of sexually coercive violence they direct toward their women. Primatologists agree that humans have no *biological* necessity to be violent to each other, but there is clear evidence that they do it anyway. Certain features present in every household and certain kinds of societies outside the homespace door condition people for greater violence against each other and especially against weaker members of the family or subgroups of the society. We will consider the internal influences in chapter seven and the shaping power of the external environment in chapter eight.

---

1 Dana Priest, "CIA Holds Terror Suspects in Secret Prisons" in Washington Post (Wednesday, November 2, 2005), confirmed by President George Bush in his address to the nation (September 6, 2006). 2 Martin N. Muller and Richard W. Wrangham, *Sexual Coercion in Primates and Humans* (Cambridge: Harvard University Press, 2009), p. 456.

CHAPTER SEVEN. PHENOMENAL TRUTH VERSUS SYSTEMIC REALITY

We have seen in the previous chapters that human nature is not simply a fundamental substance that is unambiguously good or bad. Human nature, if the concept can be said to be meaningful at all, composes a complex palette of forces that includes contradictory predispositions, some positive and nurturing, and others negative, hostile, and destructive. As far as we may state that humans have a common nature at all, we can at best say that human nature is truly Janus-faced. But its Janus face is inclined in a most ironic and dangerous way. It is doubly dangerous because while our nature predisposes us to a spectrum of dispositional potentialities, we have the overwhelming propensity to see the ingroup as righteous and irreproachable whatever harm it may do, and to see the outgroup as ill-intentioned and morally flawed whatever good they may do. This doubly distorted lens is so broadly accepted across every discipline to hold the status of an axiom in all fields of human inquiry, from neurologists to sociologists to psychologists.

Yet, the axiom flies in the face of the paradox that is the object of this study—the paradox that violence is a feature largely integral to the homespace, almost exclusively targeted on intimates and only very rarely overflowing onto external parties. People fear strangers and teach their children to avoid contact with them, but the undeniable social fact, true across all societies of the human world, is the overwhelming likelihood that when people come to be harmed, lethally or mildly, psychologically, physically, or financially, it will be at the hands of people with whom they are intimately connected. Violence is an integral feature of a great many homes around the world, regardless of race, class, or gender, ethnic, religious, or national identity.

This fact assaults our reason on a fundamental level, because home is experienced as the very place to which we retreat from the rigors of an often harsh, competitive, and threatening world. The phenomenon of home, its lived sense for human subjects, is one of refuge and security, a place where we can hang our hats, always find a welcoming embrace, get a nourishing meal and a cozy bed, and be supported in our dreams and sorrows. Home represents for most subjects the very center-point of the human world, the heart of human community, beside which all other places are measured and invariably come up wanting.

So how do we explain the glaring gap between the subjective experience of home as sanctuary and the empirical fact that disappoints the ideal, the fact that violence infects the home as a disease invades the healthy body or as a daemon invades the noble spirit? Part of the answer to this paradox must be found in the fact that homes are not only intimate phenomena constructed of emotional ties. Homes are systems. All systems are constantly in flux, changing and evolving, growing and dying. They are held in place precisely by the tension of these opposing forces, pulling inward and pushing outward. Homes are drawn toward closure in faithfulness to the fundamental mission of the home, under the explanatory rubric of serving the security of the inmates. In this whole, the parts cling to each other, draw in upon themselves, frantic for survival and desperate for reassurance against the ravages of time and the terrifying spatiality of the world. On the other hand, this very enclosing can become experienced as a suffocating grip. People need openness and space in their lives; they need new faces and fresh ideas to stimulate their growth. They need to feel that their little system fits neatly into larger networks of similar systems, where it is couched and cradled by appreciative otherness. Home dwellers need a neighborhood that welcomes their unique contribution to the tapestry of community life and values their unique input into communal projects.

The tension between openness and closure that holds the home intact is a fragile equilibrium at best. Open too wide and the system disintegrates: the world comes spilling in, defeating the intimacy of the home, revealing its secrets to forbidden eyes, and betraying its unique identity to an overwhelming difference that dilutes, confuses, and erases distinctiveness. Close too tightly and the system chokes and smothers; suffocated of the air they needs for life and alienated from the greater network of their environment, the inmates begin to turn upon each other, as prisoners confined to small, sealed cells or as rats in a tiny box. Differences are magnified in small, suffocating enclosures; everyone can begin to look like an enemy when they are always in your face.

The distorted perception of homespace vulnerability is captured in the figure of the Roman God, Janus. As the dual-visage of the ancient god demonstrates, half of the homespace smiles out to the world, while the other half fiercely glares. Friends are welcome at the gates of Rome; enemies beware. The adventuring Romans knew what the seafaring Greeks knew before them: both gods and monsters show up on the doorstep, and often they cannot be distinguished. From inside the homespace, the problem appears as the danger of open gates. Openness is perceived as a dangerous invitation to the Visigoths to ascend the twin hills. But the incidence of violence in every society indicates unequivocally that the real danger is only very rarely the external enemy. The real danger is the closedness of the gates. Anything can happen when those doors slam shut and the inmates stand outside the morally compelling eye of the society at large. The gaze of the neighbor and the ear of the passerby is what keep the homespace honest and gentle.

So the problem is a tricky one. Without the gates, the Romans cease to be Romans; with them, they are tempted to ignobility. Security and meaningful identity are purchased by the perfect tension between closing oneself off *as different* from the external, but not closing off so much that a muddied sameness crushes all vibrancy of life and difference is construed as treachery. The vitality and endurance of the system depend upon how well it holds this fragile balance, this fluid equipoise, between system integrity and member diversity, how well it manages the inner and the outer forces that constantly weigh in/out upon it, and tempt it toward violent implosion/explosion.

It is not simply that systems *cannot* thrive in isolation; they simply *do not* exist in isolation. Discrete identity and isolated existence are mere illusions that the homespace cultivates to grant identity, solidarity and intimacy. But in truth, no system is an island. There is no denying the utter embeddedness of every system within a grander schematic whole. There is no rebuffing the fact of our infinite interconnectedness with, and codependence upon, other homespaces, at every level and every site of identity formation. A tree falls in Ohio and power shuts down across the northeastern stretch of the North American continent. A Russian teen hacks into the World Wide Web and the entire global communications and financial system is threatened. A single drop of infected blood enters an open wound in some remote village in Sierra Leone and HIV threatens the continent. A system can be disrupted in an instant by a minor twist of fate; regaining the balanced integrity of the parts in the wake of system disruption can be a daunting and perhaps impossible task.

And yet this is not the final word on the matter. Systems always have points of vulnerability but they also have a way of reasserting themselves, self-generating, self-reinforcing, adapting, acclimatizing and re-proliferating. This explains why flu vaccines are always a step behind the diseases they are created to control, and why the suppression of one "terror cell" in Afghanistan gives rise to a dozen more on distant continents. External forces weigh in upon them, but systems close off quite effectively, slamming shut the doors and windows that leave them vulnerable, but opening again when the danger subsides, letting in the fresh air again and the smell of the neighbor's honeysuckle.

Human systems can be more supple and flexible than institutions and technologies. Some families crumble under tragedy, while others have a remarkable quality that sees them through the vicissitudes of life; the parts may be fragmented and broken and scarred, but still the whole somehow magically pulls itself together again. We don't know what the mysterious ingredient is that allows some families, struck down by a tragedy, to accomplish this healing feat, but there is no denying that the restorative potion is there on their pantry shelves.

More often, we observe the mystery of unfathomable system endurance in negative ways. Many of us have experienced this phenomenon: we are grown up, have gone out into the world, fashioned our own lives, designed our own operating systems according to our personal ideals and desires, and established our own traditions and rituals to maintain ourselves as independent entities. We are autonomous persons with a system of our own, with sovereign and unique identities. Or so we think. Then we go home. We hear, "You're late for dinner, dear," or "Did you forget to get a haircut?" or "You look better *today*." These phrases meet us every day in our work and personal lives and have little effect upon our well-being or self-esteem. But in our family homes, these seemingly innocent observations and questions have *special* meanings. They can be explosive, evoking long forgotten fears and anxieties, and provoking wildly defensive responses unimaginable anywhere else and unforeseeable only moments before. In our homes, these phrases send signals at a level far below the conscious; they have coded meanings within the family system that say so much more than any outsider could fathom.

A family is a system. But it is a very special kind of system. You can walk away from it, change your worldview entirely, and reconstruct your identity, perhaps explicitly charting your life's path in departure from the realities in your childhood home. But you can never resign from your family. It lays claim to you no matter how much you reject it, no matter how far away you run, demanding the fulfillment of responsibilities you have not accepted, and punishing transgressions of codes you never endorsed. Your home system remains forever a part of you and you remain a part of it.

Since our homespaces exert such enormous existential pressure upon us, the features of the home may offer us insight into the mystery of the violence that statistics locate at this intimate setting. There are a number of features that render the home vulnerable to violence. One of the crucial determining factors that positions a home for violence is its deeply embedded love of order. In every homespace, rituals proliferate to bring the di-

verse elements into common alignment. Myths then take shape
to explain and justify the rituals, trace out the margins of identity, articulate the guiding ideals and values of the order, and
assign place to the diverse elements, including rightful leaders
and heroes, and gods to oversee the entire structure. Though the
terminology of ritual and myth may sound strange applied in the
context of family identity, every homespace, at every level of human community, is a site where ritual proliferates, and where
myths arise to articulate and explain the adopted practices.

In modern social scientific studies, the terminology describing local reality postulates has shifted of late to the language of
"social construction." However, I am concerned that this language is too "active" in tone, suggesting that people consciously
go about sorting through prevailing ideas and selecting those
which work best for them. I am concerned that "construction"
suggests intentional fabrication of their common mental worlds
and self-conscious imposition of their prejudices upon their
children's minds. This simply is not how people come to their
common views and take up their shared practices.

People simply never see their prejudices *as prejudices*; they see
their truths as *the truth* and thus worthy of sharing with their
progeny. Though ideas about what constitutes truth are in constant flux and always "under construction" at every identity site,
we can state with confidence that no one is actively doing that
construction work. Rather, we are born into an already functioning worldview and the task of early life is to absorb the common ideas that pre-exist us, getting the learning right so that we
can feel we understand "the world." Those ideas only come into
view *as problematic* when and if a conflict in existing ideas con-
fronts us with a paradox that cannot be resolved or referred for
resolution to the greater wisdom of the elders or the god.

The language of "social construction," so popular in many
fields of social inquiry, has a further disadvantage. It clouds from
view a fact upon which anthropologists unanimously agree: ritual predates myth. Rituals arise to mark off the borders of identity
and distinguish the belonging from the alien, the sacred from the
profane. Only after the fact do myths bring the subtle messages
of ritual to conceptual form, filling in the conceptual spaces to
shape a worldview, the "common mental world" of the group.

All systems in the human world share broadly these ranking and ordering mechanisms that sort and make sense of the members and bring them into common alignment. Once the ranking is determined, there will be special privileges for the more valuable members, special incentives to entice lesser members to conform to the ruling logic of the system, specialized strategies of coercion to persuade the delinquent parts, special punitive sanctions to deter other members from following the poorly assimilated. There will be specialized minions to oversee the ordering processes, to monitor the functioning of the separate (lesser?) parts so that they work for the good of the whole (more valuable parts?). There will be special rituals to promote conformity and discourage deviance—prescriptions that align individual parts to the overall goals of the system and prohibitions that minimize internal conflict.

Ordering strategies and identity work, of their own accord, tend toward obsessive self-reinforcement and proliferation: identifying documents filled out in triplicate, licenses to dwell and possess, passports to monitor movement, "intelligence" strategies to track social interactions and identify signs of treachery, consensus reports to define the nature and distribution of local populations, specialized agents to anticipate external dangers and formulate the propaganda that will reinterpret homespace oppression as necessary and defensive. Ritual by ritual, triplicate form by triplicate form, the gentlest, most open system inevitably creeps toward closure. People become increasingly wedded to the ordering mechanisms that confirm the ideals, fears, aspirations, and goals of nobody in particular, but everyone in general.

Once a homespace takes shape, its conservation becomes the focus of all its energies, and the rituals of identity work struggle to accomplish the desired longevity. Stable identity requires order and ordering necessarily involves inequalities—subordinations and elevations, oppressions and oppressors. In the gentlest homes, this ordering violence may require only the imposition of a gentle discipline that suppresses wantonness and tempers excesses, granting reason the upper hand to reign in the horses of passion and appetite so that the "good life" can proceed smoothly for all members. Home-craft need not be, though it certainly can be, pathological. However, where the homespace feels itself under threat, where chaos threatens to undo stable identity, the risk increasingly escalates that identity and ordering strategies will harden into obsessive and repressive forces that suffocate the troubling diversities of the ingroup.

In a mechanical system, such as a computer, a car, or a robot, ordered integrity is certainly a desirable goal. Chaos in these kinds of systems can threaten human and other life and disrupt global communications and economies. And since systems at every level are complex, that is, composed of other, smaller systems, when one of those subsystems runs off in a chaotic direction, it takes the welfare of the larger system with it. A broken fuel pump waylays the entire vehicle; a diseased tree can infect the whole forest, if its "diversity" is not destroyed at the source. But human communities are different from mechanical systems. A family, as any system, is made up of *different* parts, but it is unrealistic and unreasonable to expect that the many differences of a human community will always be functioning in harmony. Perfect order is not only impossible in human systems; it is undesirable as a goal. In sum, the love of order that is integral to the Western worldview is an inappropriate value in the human system, at the level of family, ethnic or religious identity group, workplace community or nation.

Sadly, many households are little better than localized, culturally- and religiously-legitimated systems of oppression, where violent means (rape, prostitution, and mental and physical abuse) are called upon to serve the reigning value of maintaining the order that guarantees the continuance of the system. Once violent means are introduced and justified in the name of a shared value, such as order or god's will or patriotism, the incidence of violence in the home system becomes completely justified, because grounded in a shared moral value that has the power to trump lesser values, such as mental health or physical security.

Violence has a strong propensity to rebound from its original site and effectively and relentlessly reiterate itself in the actions of its victims. In the case of homespace violence, the rebounding is clear: one partner teaches it to each other, abused partners express their frustrations on the children or elders in the home, and older siblings dump their abjection violently upon younger siblings. Violence very effectively and openly rebounds from the top to the bottom of the system, and from generation to generation across family histories. Violence, as a matter of social scientific record, is very much a family affair.

Violence rebounds so effectively within the familial system, because relative to other integrated economic, political, and social institutions, the family home is small enough to permit a single authority, or a single style of sovereignty (patriarchal or matriarchal) to hold sway indefinitely. Though tyranny is quite rare in the world at large, coming up against multiple resistances, it is quite easily accomplished in micro-communities, such as the intimate relationship or the modern nuclear family. It is far easier to close off the familial or intimate system from the prying—and censuring—view of the larger community than it is to barricade a religious sect or political state from the purview, reproach, and reprisal of adjacent communities.

Small home units can achieve more effective closure. Closure to public view and censure favors the continuance of violent rituals, as well as the perpetuation of local myths that legitimate and re-incite the violences. Localized myths or "attribution theories" attribute culpability to the victims for the violence they undergo; they function within the repressive household to hold the abusive relationship together, ironically by *mutual* consent, through the sharing of a common mental world. Batterers tend to attribute their violences to uncontrollable events ("The situation called for a serious response") or to powerful attributes in their victims ("Her bad behavior compelled me to use force"), rather than admit their own rational/emotional dysfunction or some faulty logic in the homespace under their governance. Batterers are expert mythologizers, constructing explanations of their violence that blame the world or their victims for the abuse. These myths are powerful and compelling and are often readily adopted by the victims, which explains why so much abuse goes unreported, and why victims return again and again to the site of their abuse. Victims who flee for safety are frequently drawn back to the scene of the crime, as soon as they have regained their strength, to put right the wrong they believe themselves to have caused.

The twisted mythologies that justify intimate violence are so persistently successful in dysfunctional households because of the household's structure. Ironically, the very features that we treasure in our homes, features that render them warm, cozy, and intimate, are the same features which make the home the likeliest site for the eruption of violence. The fact that a home is cherished as a private, enclosed space, where secrets can be shared without risking public display, also leaves homes vulnerable to intimate abuse.

I have said that much of the violence, in human relations in general and in family relations in particular, is rooted in the fact of institutionalization, in its structure as a functioning system. From an evolutionary standpoint, inequalities in systems provide a hefty benefit, spurring the advance of a species. Rankings are what permit higher vertebrates to evolve as systems, politically, economically, and socially. Status distinctions and role differentiations order the network of differing talents and capacities, streamline functionality, and purchase solidarity against external threats. Inequalities in status, rights, and powers are endorsed and experienced as desirable by most members of the system, because distinctions are the crux of individual identity and give a sense of meaningful existence, and they establish a clear path for ascending the social and political ladder. Thus it is that precisely those members who are most oppressed by the system who are often the most fervent supporters of the system's hierarchy of distinctions. For who so desperately craves a clear path for elevation than the politically and socially inferior? If the mythology is well entrenched, as in the case of the American Dream myth, it will indefinitely hold intact the most exploitative, least socially mobile, system, keeping the under-rewarded laboring without complaint for shamelessly low minimum wages, and even inspiring them to rally to the support of tax breaks for the super-rich because they fervently believe that *anyone* can climb to the top of the social and political ladder, with enough hard work and passion.

Rankings and orderings are the means to system success; they serve the solidarity of the system and they generally serve the interests of those in control of the system. In the family system, the goals of the parents may well align with the best interests of the lesser household members, and sometimes the power structure is flipped upside down and the interests and desires of the children are the primary focus of the parents. The value of the system's ranking and ordering structure is determined by the value of the criteria and methods people use to ascend the system. If the system grants positive rewards (extended curfew, extra TV time) for positive individual achievement (a strong school report card, doing the dishes) gained by appropriate means (study, volunteerism), then the system is exercising a healthy rewards structure that serves positive values, establishes a clear path for advancement, and encourages emulation instead of resentment. But if the system rewards inappropriate behaviors (fighting at school, ducking out on chores), it affirms destructive values (aggression, irresponsibility), and sets a bad example to other members.

In ordered systems, institutionalized inequalities can constrict or misdirect individual development. One way a system achieves this is by categorizing members in ways that limit their access to responsibilities and rewards. Assigned categories that confine the members to given ranks and roles include age, gender, birthplace in the family, or sheer favoritism. Institutionalized inequalities are grounded in meaning categories that are historically and ethnically or religiously grounded. Consigned roles and ranks grow inflexible over time, and increasingly constraining to those so assigned, so the most ostensibly benign categorizations (oldest oversees younger siblings) can elicit resentment from those it confines, if inadequate rewards repay desired behaviors.

Rankings and orderings tend to trigger resentments and frustrations in the family home. In many homes, a single leader stands at the top of the system, enjoying the final word on decisions that inevitably affect every member. So there is plenty of room for dissatisfaction all the way down the system hierarchy. Though tyranny is more easily achievable in the micro-system of the family than in a broader environment, the home leader need not be flagrantly tyrannical for the system to weigh heavily upon ingroup members. Simone Weil writes poignantly of the effect that all human beings, however benign, exert upon one another by virtue of their sheer proximity.

The human beings around us exert just by their presence a power which belongs uniquely to themselves to
stop, to diminish, or modify any movement which our
bodies design. A person who crosses our path does not
turn aside our steps in the same manner as a street sign,
no one stands up or moves about, or sits down in quite
the same fashion when he is alone in a room as when he
has a visitor.[1]

The most benign presence limits those in proximity by exert-
ing a weight upon their freedom that cannot be readily deflected
or ignored. But where the presence is less than benign, the influence can be crushing. Weil goes on to describe how severe
coercion transforms victims in their very substance:

These are not men living harder lives than others,
not placed lower socially than others, these are another
species, a compromise between a man and a corpse.
That a human being should be a thing is, from the point
of view of logic, a contradiction. But when the impossible has become a reality, a contradiction is as a rent in
the soul. That thing aspires at every moment to become
a man and never at any moment succeeds.[2]

Weil illuminates how the most suffocating forms of tyranny
transform its victims. But she limits the effects of tyranny to the
destruction of human will and spirit. She fails to follow the reboundings of tyranny down the logical trail of its effects. In general, the disempowered are not merely powerless and crushed
by their experiences, not merely apathetic and "thing-like." Human beings may be momentarily crushed but as a rule, they are
enormously resilient. They ultimately emerge from this soul-
crushing, but not without having been permanently altered in
more dangerous respects than Weil allows. The human spirit
rebounds from oppression, and rebounding victims are dangerous. Social and psychological scientists tell us that the disempowered are the time-bombs of their societies, ticking away in

1 Simone Weil. *Intimations of Christianity Among the Ancient Greeks.*
Elizabeth Chase Geissbuhler, ed. and trans. (London: Routledge and
Kegan Paul, 1976), pp. 24-55, p. 28.
2 Ibid., p. 28.

their resentment to a final, violent explosion of their abjection and frustration.[1]

Weil's description of the victim of tyranny aligns with the popular view of "victim" as unambiguously *innocent* and *powerless* recipient of abuse. Certainly the most common victims of intimate abuse are the least powerful in the family—poor, uneducated women and children—and their powerlessness in the family is complemented by their powerlessness in the society at large, a double guarantee of voicelessness. Victims, trapped in abusive relationships, *feel* very palpably their powerlessness because very often they *are* trapped—physically, economically, emotionally, and culturally. Those who do try to escape the trap learn quickly that violence often follows them in their retreat. The abuse not only often continues, but quite frequently increases in frequency and intensity *after separation*, with 75 percent of emergency room visits by battered women occurring in the post-separation period.[2]

The fact that victims are often hopelessly trapped in situations of abuse, however, does not rule out their propensity to become mediums for the rebounding of violence. In fact, in households where one member is bullied and abused, it is quite common to find violence traveling down the chain of power, assuming new forms and targets all down the length of the chain. A man beats his wife, the wife beats her children, and the older siblings beat the younger ones, who turn and kick the dog. When violence visits the family home, it tends to begin at the top, then make the full round of the family.

I have stated that the home is predisposed toward violence because of its institutional structure and its size relative to other systems. But there are a number of features *internal* to the family home that situate it as a site for violence. One of the most important of these internal features is the fact that family life involves, and indeed *requires* of its members, deep emotive investment in shared interactions. The member's failure to make that investment is considered a fundamental failing. We are *required* to care

---

1 Rollo May. *Power and Innocence* (New York: Norton & Co., 1972).
2 The statistics in this chapter have been supplied by National Clearinghouse for the Defense of Battered Women, Philadelphia (www.ncdbw.org retrieved March 14, 2013).

about the joys, sorrows, and achievements of each ingroup member, as well invest in shared projects, such as family vacations. We must care fervently about these things, or we are judged—by ourselves and by others—as inadequately committed. But precisely because so many individual and joint projects contend for sustained attention and emotional investment, energies can run high at the home site, and people can be drawn thin by the plethora of demands upon their limited emotional energy.

Where there is inadequate attention to go around, ingroup members may become supportive, siblings stepping in to cover for busy parents in tending the younger and needier. But the general disposition in an environment where there is not quite enough attention to go around is for each member to close off around their personal interests and compete, rather than cooperate, with the others. Pitted against each other in contests for limited accolades, members often wallow in feelings of neglect, indignity, and inadequacy, while the struggling parent(s) juggling everyone's demands for attention experience feelings of inadequacy and failure for their inability to fill all demands and meet everyone's expectations of high emotional investment in each and every project and person.

Since there is high emotional investment in the network of relationships at the home site, there is also a high propensity for the varied emotive responses to flare out of control. This is one of the primary reasons why violence is a regular visitor to the homespace, even—and perhaps especially—where ideals of support and nurture are highest. One cannot run at high intensity and broad emotional spread across a number of people, projects and interests, without regular outbursts of emotional catharsis.

Even where the familial system is not rigorously hierarchical and adult authorities are open to negotiation in decision-making circumstances, there is always uneven negotiating expertise between adults and children, boys and girls, older and younger siblings. Moreover, many of the activities families share tend to be inherently conflict-structured, and differences in age, gender, levels of development, and arenas of talent widen the potential for conflict across generations and genders. Therefore, however benign the rules governing group interactions, the likelihood that decisions will suit all parties is understandably slim. Often the rules are exceedingly simple—*respect for elders* and *give in to the youngest*—but even these broad guidelines can be divisive because they protect the interests of the few. Reductive protections may be experienced as unfair by the "middle folk" of the ingroup, as the decisions of everyday life (what to watch on television, what's for dinner, and when is bedtime) come to be decided by reference to them ("We'll eat when your father gets home!" or "Let your sister watch Sesame Street!"). The most benign regulations that protect some members also betray other members, and they frame all decision-making as win/lose situations, in which individuals have unequal claims to the benefits of the system.

Another aspect of family life that predisposes it to negative emotive response is the general assumption that members have the right to interfere in each other's affairs. Family intimates necessarily share an extensive knowledge of everyone else's personal and social biographies. In the close quarters of the family home, it can be devastating to carry on daily activities with everyone knowing, judging, and recalling ad infinitum every mistake, every failure, and every inadequacy. Though all human beings crave intimacy, group intimacy often conflicts with individual needs for privacy. Members can feel that their secrets and vulnerabilities are constantly and nakedly paraded before the entire group, even when no mention of the individual's failure is publicly expressed. We all, from time to time, find the intimacy of family relations suffocating. We find ourselves wishing to opt out and retire to a more private setting, where we can commit our inevitable errors, nurse our wounds, and plot our future courses, in greater anonymity. But family membership is involuntary and interminable. We can break out, leave the house, and refuse to return, but we can never be free of their influence.

Familial influence is unrelenting because family relations are secured through personal, social, material, and legal commitments, all of which comfort group members *from within* but can serve as entrapments when one is seeking to depart the family embrace. When conflicts arise, giving up one's membership is not as easy as resigning from a voluntary social organization. This is no small disincentive to escape, not even for the battered partner, who may have great difficulty putting personal safety ahead of her family obligations. Deserting family responsibilities, abandoning loved ones, and breaking up the family is a moral burden that many victims are unwilling to bear.

Finally, a feature of the home predisposing it for intimate violence is the vulnerability of human beings to stress in times of change. Change is inevitable within families. Births, deaths, adolescence, aging, job loss or promotion, retirement, moving, illness, bad grades, learning to drive, leaving for college—all these varied circumstances and episodes of family life bring new challenges and frustrations, that must be borne, negotiated, and worked through by every member of the family. In times of economic pressures, such as the current economic "down-turn" when the entire globe is undergoing significant change for the worse, it is not the corrupt politicians, greedy bankers, or single-minded CEOs who pay the price for the mess that they have made. It is the family that suffers job loss, erosion of savings, loss of homes, and bankruptcy. These tragedies do not have to befall a family; the mere threat of their occurrence is enough to wear down member nerves, and leave everyone just a little more emotionally volatile than they are in better times.

We have seen in the previous chapters that the contradictory impulses embedded in human nature exist not as determinative forces, but as mere potentialities, waiting to be triggered by factors in the environment. The fact that our impulses are contradictory dictates that we must take care with people's environments, assuring that everyone has an adequate share of the resources that sustain life and grant security, so as to promote the positive qualities that broaden our empathy and deactivate the negative, mind-narrowing qualities that split the world into friend and foe. The insecure environment is the dehumanizing environment, which nurtures the destructive, xenophobic aspect of our human nature.

The environments that seem to be capable of affecting us most deeply are those of our early life, when we are most vulnerable to imprinting. The experiences we have in early years can poise us for good or ill, framing the world as a half-full or half-empty glass. Childhood experiences prepare us for a lifetime of happiness and goodwill or plant deep-seated feelings of inadequacy, resentment, and shame that will eventually find their way to the surface for release in emotive catharsis. Psychologists who treat violent offenders identify a single common attribute among these perpetrators—common negative experiences in their early life. They have either suffered severe neglect or maltreatment by authority figures, usually a father, stepfather, or uncle, or they have witnessed the abuse of a loved one, usually a mother or a sibling. The experiences themselves may be long forgotten, repressed in the depths of the mind and embedded in the psyche.

What has only recently been studied and identified is the fact that these destructive affects—fear, shame, guilt, self-loathing, distrust, and rage—drive victims in one of two directions. They may accept the world as a terrifying place where only the strong survive, brace themselves against it, and project their shame and rage onto loved ones or in rarer cases, strangers. On the other hand, the survivors of childhood abuse may be left with low self-esteem, feeling deserving of the abuse they suffered or witnessed as children. These victims have a strong likelihood in later life of seeking out abusive relationships, to return to the scene of the crime, so to speak, to correct the dysfunctional relationship. In a highly controversial break-through study, Linda G. Mills asks the forbidden question—what is it about the victims that drives them to return to abusive relationships? It has long been impermissible to ask questions about the identity of victims, because it suggests that victims are implicated in the causes of abuse, challenging the notion of the pure victim. For the same reasons, feminists and psychologists have rejected the idea of couples counseling for cases involving intimate violence. Mills' controversial study does just these two taboo things—asks about the victim's participation in the violence dynamic and counsels both victim and abuser, as well as the extended family and community, regarding how to dismantle the dynamic. Mills concludes that victims of intimate abuse often submit to a partner's violence, because they see it as a fresh opportunity to reclaim their self-worth and salvage the love they were denied by a neglectful parent.[1]

A great deal of research has been conducted to clarify much of the mystery about violent perpetrators. However, until Mills'

---

1 Linda G. Mills, *Violent Partners* (New York: Basic Books, 2008).

study, very little investigation has inquired into what drives victims to return again and again to abusive relationships. This research paucity makes perfect sense, given the Western understanding of intimate violence. The accepted model for understanding intimate abuse is very simple and unambiguous: an aggressive, bullying male attacks a submissive, innocent female. In this model, episodes of violence have a single cause, the aggression of the perpetrator, and are expressed onto a hapless and helpless victim, who is utterly blameless. Therefore, it is standard practice *not* to study the victim, not to identify any characteristics in the victim as pertinent to the abuse, since this would amount to blaming the victim for contributing to her own abuse.

Thus until very recently therapists refused to ask the questions whose answers would let them see that violence is rarely a unilateral force that arises *ex nihilo* and moves unilaterally. Violence is generally a power and affect dynamic, a kind of dance, in which two or more people engage, often following predictable patterns of escalation and emotive release in which both parties participate, at least in the early stages of the dynamic until the frustration level of the dominant partner reaches the breaking point and more serious harm doing is called upon to end the spiraling situation.

In this chapter, we have seen that the humiliations and abuses of childhood are carried along through a person's life, and are imported into their homes at all levels of identity work. Traditions of childrearing and patterns of intimate relations tend to be carried over from generation to generation, and while it is not the case that every beaten child grows up to beat his own wife and children, it is the case that in a high percentage of cases where spouses and parents abuse their loved ones, the perpetrators turn out to have been victims of abuse in childhood. Victimhood does not *determine* perpetration; we can break the violence tradition, reject the injustice we have suffered, and put our experience and knowledge to good use in developing healthier coping mechanisms to get us through stressful circumstances. Victimhood is no viable excuse for perpetration, but it is a very common constant.

It is fair to assume that no person consciously approaches the world with the objective of doing harm to others, least of all their intimate loved ones. But precisely because violence is a time-honored ordering mechanism, many people are able to discount their harm doing in the name of a great value, social order. Ironically, many religions promote the value of violence as an ordering mechanism in the home. In general, the more blindly religious people are, the quicker they are to justify the use of violence, condoning it as effective and necessary to the higher value of order.[1] This explains why fervently religious folk are quick to endorse war, severe punishments, and the death penalty. Most religions hold a theory of history that affirms suffering as the means to salvation, so it is difficult to convince people under the thrall of this belief that violence is always wrong and suffering should be eliminated. God is in charge of the madhouse, they claim, and will be using his own violences in the fullness of time to take his revenge on infidels.

"Spare the rod and spoil the child" voices the belief in the efficacy of violence in the nursery. No matter how many therapists deny the value of corporal and psychological punishment and warn of the long term effects of these harms, parents (and very often religious parents) continue to cling with desperation to their "right" to physically and psychologically abuse their youngsters. It is no great leap for a parent who applies physical and emotional punishment for children to justify similar abuses to the spouse. Indeed in societies such as the United States and Britain, whose armed forces are daily punishing new "infidels" in some far corner of the globe, violence is an integral feature of the societal worldview, seen to serve as a valuable ordering mechanism. For people under the thrall of this militaristic worldview, it is a very small leap, when intimates fall out of line, to bring them back into step with a taste of the fist, the boot or the gun.

Violence occurs in over half of American homes, with comparable frequency and brutality across all social classes and all ethnic groups. In a shocking number of families, physical abuse is part of the daily routine of family life, from spanking to kicks, bites, and punches.[2] These figures, while distressing, do not in-

---

1 James A. Haught, *Holy Hatred: Religious Conflicts of the 1990s* (New York: Prometheus Books, 1994).
2 Mary Lystad. *Violence in the Home: Interdisciplinary Perspectives* (Philadelphia: Brunner-Routledge, 1986).

dicate a new phenomenon; family violence has been a problem as long as there have been families. Centuries ago, John Stuart Mill lamented this fact in his essay "On the Subjection of Women":

> However brutal a tyrant she may be chained to—
> though she may know that he hates her, though it may
> be his daily pleasure to torture her, and though she
> may feel it impossible not to loathe him—he can claim
> from her and enforce the lowest degradation of a hu-
> man being, that of being made the instrument of an
> animal function contrary to her inclinations... When we
> consider how vast is the number of men, in any great
> country, who are little more than brutes, and that this
> never prevents them from being able, through the laws
> of marriage, to obtain a victim, the breadth and depth of
> human misery caused in this shape alone by the abuse of
> the institution swells to something appalling.[1]

Intimate violence has always existed, but people simply closed their eyes to it across much of history, under the convic-tion that the private life of families is not the business of outsid-ers. Thus the severity of the problem of intimate violence only began to emerge into the public consciousness in the 1960s, beginning with the recognition of the vast numbers of children who were showing up in emergency rooms, obvious victims of abuse. Finally, after pediatric radiologists made public the num-ber of broken bones children were suffering, "battered children syndrome" was addressed as a societal problem. Over the next decade, concern expanded to embrace battered wives. Elder abuse came to light much more recently, along with premarital intimate battering and "date rape" violence.

Research indicates that men are overwhelmingly the per-petrators of intimate battering and women and children over-whelmingly the victims. However the cycles of violence that lead up to physical assaults tend to include spiraling acts of aggression from both parties. Men do not have a monopoly on violence but when they do snap, their abuse tends to be physi-cal, whereas women resort to the more subtle weaponry of psy-

1 Cited by Lystad, *Violence in the Home*, pp. 30-36.

chological and verbal aggression, which to be sure, can be even more deeply wounding than physical beatings, but leaves fewer visible signs. Little research has been performed in analyzing the spirals of intimate violence because the notion that violence is cyclical, and not a simple unilateral phenomenon, still meets with fierce resistance in the community of professional therapists who treat intimate violence.

Over the past sixty years, attitudes, sensibilities, gender roles, public expectations and awareness have dramatically evolved. Women have come forth from their kitchens, won control over their bodies through new methods of birth control, and have taken their places in the workforce. This change has enormously affected their power quotient, both in their families and in society in general. Recent generations of old world cultures that were traditionally rigorously patriarchal have begun to come around to new, more enlightened ideals. In many households, it is women who compose the economic and social powerhouse.

With the good news of increasing female empowerment come traces of the dark side of power: we are beginning to hear more frequently of female violence toward their male partners. Though little research has directly targeted the problem, what we do know is troubling: female battering of male partners is both coming out of the closet and increasing every year. As more and more cases of male partner abuse hit the media and filter down onto television "talk shows" and reality shows, the public are increasingly forced to admit that the traditional simplistic model—*aggressive male victimizes innocent and submissive female*—no longer reflects the reality. Few women are simply "innocent and submissive victims" and many males are increasingly emasculated by the shifting power structure of Western societies.

Thus we may assert that the gender identity of the intimate abuser is less assured than it used to be. However, coercive methods employed to achieve order in the household will vary less with gender than with the dominant partner's cultural and religious orientation and her view of the state of security in the family. Socio-cultural factors can provide justifications for abuse, can also construe partner control as care, and equate gender with fitness for specified roles. Moreover, industrialized societies present increasingly grave pressures to the homespace.

Western societies are rigorously hierarchical, placing high value on independence, autonomy, and self-reliance; in turn these factors promote blind respect for authority and uncritical acceptance of coercive mechanisms of control of weaker members. Unqualified valuations of authority convince both the powerless and the powerful that force is a legitimate means of maintaining social order.

If the function of intimate societies is to nurture, support, and protect inmates, as it is *intuitively felt* to be, then the violence that characterizes all too many Western homes is incompatible with the home's felt function. We imagine homespace violence to be anomalous, a glitch in an otherwise healthy system. But, sadly, violence is far too frequent a visitor in the family home to permit us to label it a stranger, who infrequently passes by. The fact is that homespace violence fits exceedingly well within the logic of the brave new world of hyper-capitalism. Degraded marketplace values of profit and expedience shape people to push others out of their way as they race to their private fortunes. It is not always easy for people to leave those self-serving values at work at the end of the day. The home's aspect of gentle nurturance can easily be betrayed, and the happiness of individual members can quickly be forgotten, when homes are bent to the logic of a larger dehumanizing system. In the next chapter we will consider in detail how homespace values are shaped and molded by the degraded values of industrialization and consumerism in the era of late capitalism.

CHAPTER EIGHT. SYSTEMS WITHIN VIOLENT SYSTEMS

We have seen in the previous chapter that many integral features of home position it for conflict situations, and because the home is an intimate site of human dwelling, the conflict-structured activities among intimates tend to involve very high stakes (self-esteem, feeling favored or neglected by loved ones) and also very high stress, due to the suffocating closeness of the intimate space. We saw too that home is a system, albeit a system of a peculiar form. Systems maintain order and advance in their society by organizing around a common logic. Family systems teach that logic to their members through family rituals—from everyday routines around sharing of food and access to attention or benefits, to strategies of response to misdemeanor and security crisis. The organizing logic of the homespace, being a sacred space of human dwelling, is often cherished by the inmates and taken for granted as right and inviolable, even under radically evolving—or devolving—circumstances. Because the learning that takes place at the homespace often happens through mindless ritual, not rational deliberation, the learning is mostly pre-rational, occurring at a subliminal level.

Thus it is no surprise to learn that the logic of homes quite effectively reproduces itself in the mindset and worldview of future generations—sometimes in departure from those rituals found to be objectionable, but very often in faithfulness to the logic of home. This explains why victims of homespace violence often fail to learn the lessons their experiences should have taught them—that violence is destructive of homespace bonds and harms everyone it touches, often for life. Research into intimate violence unequivocally demonstrates that perpetrators of intimate violence have themselves suffered from that destructive plague during their own youth or witnessed such violence being perpetrated upon another intimate, while they were forced to stand by helplessly watching.

Homes are systems. Systems operate according to a certain logic and maintain ritual practices that reinforce that logic. When the logic becomes skewed to legitimate violence against inmates or outgroups, the fallout can be highly destructive. Sometimes a maladaptive logic has its origins within the homespace in prejudice or low self-esteem promoted by the leaders. But often the source of the pathology is broader than the single home. Family systems are embedded within larger systems, and as such, that they are deeply affected by the logic of those larger systems.

Patriarchy decisively shifts the logic for homespace dwelling. According to Muller and Wrangham:

> [W]herever women lack social power, control, and authority, and are regarded as inferior to men . . . men [use their greater power to control women for reproductive purposes but they] can also use their patriarchal power to control women's sexuality for nonreproductive purposes, such as political goals.[1]

Under Pakistani law, at least four adult male Muslim witnesses must witness the act of penetration for rape to be established. Where such heavy witnessing is lacking, the rape victim may be accused of having had consensual sex and may be charged with adultery, the legal penalty for which is public stoning or whipping.

In societies under the influence of extreme patriarchal ideologies, nearly total female submission to male coercion exists. In

1 Muller and Wrangham, *Sexual Coercion in Primates and Humans*, pp. 457-58.

such societies, female genital mutilation (clitorectomy, excision, and infibulation) is widespread, as it is among Arab Muslims of the Sudan's Nile Valley, and these practices are rigorously overseen, defended, policed, and perpetuated by women, especially the grandmothers. "In such cases, male power is so pervasive that women preemptively facilitate men's coercive tactics."[1]

In states at war and around military bases of all nations, rape and gang rape rates soar. Sometimes rape is promoted by military leaders as a tool of terror and sometimes it is employed to "teach women lessons about the power of men."[2] One striking example comes from the Boulia district of Queensland, Australia:

> [A] pubescent girl is caught by a number of men; they forcibly enlarge the vaginal orifice by tearing it downward with their fingers, which have possum twine wound round them, then [they] have sexual relations with her, collecting the semen and drinking it ritually.[3]

As disturbing as this example is, cruel treatment of women is not confined to exotic tribal societies. In 1997, 88,000 men were incarcerated in U.S. prisons for violent sexual offenses, though this is only the tip of a massive iceberg of sexual abuse against women, as the vast majority of rapes go unreported. Social and political relations in the society at large shape homely spaces for peaceful or violent modes of dwelling. In this chapter, we will turn to Conflict Theory to help us understand the shaping effect that differing politico-economic forms have upon human behaviors.

In the past half century, a great deal of knowledge has been accumulated through the comparative and theoretical analysis of conflicts. Conflict study has helped to create an arsenal of expertise that can now be reapplied to new conflict zones and new conflict parties, to help people heal from their abjection and to more effectively resolve differences with their intimates and neighbors, before their conflict flares into the bloody battlefield

---

1 Ibid., p. 263.
2 Ibid., p.460.
3 Ibid. Citing R. M. Berndt and C. H. Berndt, *The World of the First Australians* (Canberra: Aboriginal Studies Press, 1988), p. 181.

of open conflict.

Though every conflict is utterly unique in its motivating goals, its politico-historico-economic circumstances, the types of conflict it adopts, and its rebounding effects, experts have learned a great deal about common features of conflict, which they have then come to apply in highly practical and innovative ways. The more we have come to know about conflict, the better we understand how to identify potential sites of conflict, understand conflict goals, track the life cycle of conflict, predict the risk potential for further episodes of violence, mediate to avoid future conflict, and help people to move forward from negative histories to overcome their legacies of violence.

This collective knowledge and expertise has proven enormously beneficial. But the benefits come with much paradox. First, much of this invaluable research necessarily hails from countries that enjoy the prosperity, hence the leisure time and the safe distance from open conflict, that grants the luxury of reflection. In short, prosperous Western nations are fast becoming experts in solving other people's problems. Peacebuilding commissions from developed countries make practical use of conflict expertise, counseling brown-skinned peoples of developing societies on the far side of the globe about how to be more like them—peaceful, prosperous, and focused upon economic development instead of other rivalries.[1]

Many Westerners believe we rightfully own civilized solutions to conflict, since, they argue, Western industrialized nations stand at the apex of human civilization. This is no novel worldview, but comes to us by way of Enlightenment philosophies such as Hegel's unfolding Reason, with its racist overtones, and Social Darwinist categorizations of human societies, that grant superiority to Western "civilized" societies. There exists deep irony in the fact that Westerners emerge as the cham-

---

1 The line-up of conflict theorists reflect this dichotomy: Max Gluckman (1911-1975) and John Rex (1925-...) in the U.K., Lewis A. Coser (1913-2003) and Randall Collins (1941-...) in the United States, and Ralf Dahrendorf (1929-...) in Germany hail from the tradition of Ludwig Gumplowicz (1838-1909), Vilfredo Pareto (1848-1923), Georg Simmel (1858-1918), Karl Marx (1818-1883) and Max Weber (1864-1920). Otomar Bartos and Johan Galtung labor in public and private sectors of the world to bring practical applications of conflict theory to mediate in conflicts around the globe.

pions of peace. The irony resides in the fact of the overwhelming imperialistic violence that brought us to the prosperity that affords us our reflective leisure.

If conflict theory has taught us anything, its lessons include the fact that no modern-day conflicts rival the sweeping atrocities of imperialism. But it also teaches us that violence does not simply disappear when we pack up our empires and return to our mother countries. Violence has an enormous propensity to rebound across historical and geographical landscapes. Victims become perpetrators. The West has left behind so many victims on its march to global economic hegemony that violence continues to rebound in distant corners of the globe, as a result of our past interventions there, creating the very conflicts that we send out our experts to cure.

Violence stays long in victim societies and bends them, both conceptually and militarily, in the direction of violence. But violence also remains with perpetrator communities long after the open conflict subsides. Reboundings of violence tend to become more cunning and insidious over time, become embedded in systems and cultural institutions, and shape future generations to trust in the efficacy of violence for order and the necessity of violence for defense. Conflict theory helps us to understand the conditions that promote violence, the harms that radical violence effects upon both perpetrator and victim groups, and the slippery slope that divides the two identity categories of victim and perpetrator. It teaches us the rebounding nature of violence, its tendency to become embedded in knowledge systems and cultural institutions, and its propensity to sublimate into insidious forms over time.

Conflict Theory in a Nutshell

Conflict theory rests upon the assumption that a continual struggle exists between different aspects of any society, as people compete for social status and access to power and social benefits (money, leisure, sexual partners, or, in worst cases, the simple necessities of life). There are a few basic conflicts (gender, race, ethnicity) but the primary social conflict is that of class. Since inequalities in power and benefits are built into all social structures, the class with the most power seeks to conserve the status quo of power relations, while those deprived of system benefits seek to bring about change; some (Marx) say abrupt and revolutionary change, others, change by democratic process.

Conflict theory essentially conforms to the classic pyramidal understanding of power as top-down, coercive structural dominance, in which an elite dictates the terms of social relations to the masses. All major institutions, laws, and traditions in the society are created to ensure the longevity of the society, with the express intent of supporting the status quo of power relations. Moral ideas about good and bad, virtue and vice, and by extension sociological definitions of normalcy and deviance, attitudes toward crime, and penal policy also support the status quo of power relations. The ideas of the ruling class form the ruling ideas of the society. Anything that challenges the control of the elites of the society will likely be considered deviant and morally reprehensible.

Conflict theory seeks to catalogue the ways in which those in power seek to stay in power, and the ways that subordinates seek to change or overthrow the system that oppresses them. It reports that different classes employ different modes of conflict, from the indirect violences of social dominance, structural inequalities, and worker and student strikes to the direct violences of warfare and violent revolution. All classes, they say, develop self-justifying ideologies that promote their peculiar interests, and justify their peculiar violences. Higher classes tend to hold more abstract ideologies, while those of subordinated classes usually reflect the want and deprivation that characterize their lives. However, both powerful and disempowered often see human nature as flawed, self-serving, and naturally aggressive, and violence as an unfortunate but functional and necessary proponent of order or historical change.

Conflicted Social Realities

Industrial Societies

One of the most common arguments rallied in favor of the currently globalizing "free trade" industrial-military-consumerist system of "elite globalization" is that along with commodities, technologies, and expertise, freedom, democracy, and liberal values are being exported across the globe. Western, industrialized, capitalist democracies, the argument runs, are the only societies that enjoy freedom, peace, and prosperity, are self-governed through participatory democracy, and share liberal values (gender equality, religious freedom, freedom of thought and speech, limits on government intrusion into individual private affairs, and fair laws and balanced systems of justice, grounded in private property rights and social contracts equalizing individual powers).

In the developed nations of the West, individual freedom, citizen equality, human dignity, and democratic representation are considered axiomatic. Thus, one might well expect less class conflict in these societies, as its ideology is promotes individual success and opportunity. We might expect greater fraternity among their populations as they share common favorable living standards. We might expect certain desirable features to be generally shared among the populations of these fortunate nations: they should prove to be broadminded, tolerant and appreciative of social differences, noninterventionist with regard to their neighbors and other nations, freethinking, well-informed, and progressive in their politics. Most of all, Western societies, committed as they are to liberal values, should stand firm in their support of human freedom and their opposition to policies and practices of coercion.

Experts in conflict theory, however, note quite the opposite features in the populations of industrialized societies. Otomar Bartos, one of the notable pioneers of applied conflict theory, highlights the tendency of industrial societies to produce alienated, isolated, hyper-competitive individuals who seek personal gain over communal benefits, care little about their neighbors, and are quick to abandon even their familial ties and social responsibilities in pursuit of private gain.[1] In short, citizens of industrialized nations tend to be greedy and selfish, and do not play well with others.

The fact is that individuals tend to reflect the characteris-

---

1 Otomar Bartos and Paul Weir, *Using Conflict Theory* (Cambridge University Press, 2002).

tics and the values of the system in which they are immersed. Since industrial societies are grounded in a capitalist utilitarian pragmatism, their ethos is one of cost-effectiveness, efficiency, and productivity. These systems, which Bartos names "vertically differentiated power hierarchies," mold citizens in the direction of the capitalist ethos, rendering them instrumentalist, profit-seeking, hyper-rationalized, atomistic, bureaucratic, detached from their fellow citizens, and unfeeling of other's sufferings.

The whole-part influence (from system to citizen) enjoys profound effects for two distinct reasons. First, Western systems, though named "democratic," are rigorously plutocratic; that is, as suggested by Bartos' nomenclature, they are vertically hierarchized according to socio-economic distinctions and governed by those enjoying a disproportionate share of the national wealth. Class differentiation within hierarchical systems is rigorously vertical, and tends to create situations where individuals are thrown into direct competition with each other over "incompatible goals." In these contests, individuals come out winners or losers, that is, their interactions amount to the most serious kind of conflict situations—"zero sum games." Though anthropologists assure us that human beings have an equally strong drive toward cooperation as toward aggression, when people find themselves in vertical hierarchies that offer little relief from the intense competition that pits each against the others and leaves scores of failures for every rare win, the cooperation predisposition is bound to fall away in favor of the aggression predisposition that favors success.

Indeed this suspicion is confirmed in a famed article in *The Nation* (dated November 21, 1994). Here Art Hilgart describes a disquieting phenomenon that he names "The Unscrupulousness Quotient." Opposing UQ to IQ, Hilgart argues:

> A chronic puzzle confronting world-betterers through the ages is why some people achieve material success while others lead nasty, brutish and short lives of quiet desperation. In recent years, systematic evidence compiled by social scientists has supported a novel hypothesis that the difference is genetic. In longitudinal studies of thousands of lives, using statistical

techniques that hold constant such variables as environment, family status and measured I.Q., the critical factor may have been isolated. That factor has been provisionally named the "unscrupulousness quotient."

What the UQ means in practical terms is that people caught up in the logic of their system in win or lose contests ("zero sum games") have learned to fight dirty with their neighbors. In modern industrial society, we have grown quite comfortable stepping on others' fingers as we clamber up the ladder of success.[1]

Fighting dirty pays dividends of success within the system, so unscrupulous behaviors are rewarded and reinforced, replicated by protégés, and openly cultivated across winning communities. But even beyond people's work lives, the marketplace ethos takes firm grip. Hilgart insists that the UQ critical factor in success is genetic, but nature and nurture are at work here. The successful in systems teach their skills to their children and pass their genes on to their progeny, and thus unscrupulous behaviors become doubly reinforced across generations. Nature and nurture work hand in hand in families, societies, and systems, exemplifying winning behaviors at home, and, at an ever-increasing rate in a globalizing world, exporting those behaviors across the globe.

The second reason that vertically-hierarchical systems enjoy a profound effect upon their members is that individuals, once pitted against each other, tend to strategize, in the logic of the system, how best to adapt and excel in their environments. Thus, in industrial societies, people organize for individual success along the industrial model: they extract raw energies from their environments, translate human assets into usable, marketable commodities, rank and value commodities according to their short-term profitability (rather than according to long-term benefits such as social harmony or sustainability), organize themselves for profit (rather than for the cultivation of individual virtues or the good of society), and distribute their resources only for profit (to the ruin of human rights and communal

---

1 The image of struggling competitors recalls the myth of the Feast of Being from Plato's *Phaedrus* 246-249, where Plato attributes the loss of human "wings" and their fall from heaven to their *phthonos* (greed, competitiveness, envy).

responsibility), managing the whole operation of their lives in desensitized, routinized, bureaucratic, industrial fashion—rationally, not emotively or compassionately. The organizing logic of the marketplace reproduces itself in the individual, rendering each affectively-neutral, self-promoting, achievement-oriented, skill-specific, grimly technical, fiercely competitive—in short, dehumanized.

The whole affects the elements which compose it, but the influence also runs in the contrary direction. Markets dictate the shape of systems; systems shape their populations; populations in turn reinforce the logic of the system by reflecting its logic in their daily affairs.[1] All around and up and down, human values are eroded and market system values embraced. The more ethically sensitive cogs in the system will try to salvage their private values by compartmentalizing the conflicted aspects of their lives. For an extreme example of values compartmentalization, consider the highly cultured private lives of the Nazi officers vis-à-vis the heartless brutality of their work lives, poignantly evidenced in the design of the concentration camp, with its factories running night and day and its stark dormitories stuffed with emaciated laborers, edged by grand Nazi family homes of exquisite beauty and refinement. The Nazi commandant, passing through the gates and into the prison yard, would adjust his character to meet the rigors of his public charge, and then would pass back again to his family home and become in his private affairs quite some other character—a loving husband and a doting father.

We witness more and more this values-compartmentalization as the logic of the market increasingly eats into people's daily lives. Consider the popularity of expressions such as "business is business" and "we are in business to make a profit, not friends." A mentor once described his shopkeeper father to me in the following terms: "You will like him, Wendy; he is generous and warm—except in business, in which case, he drains

---

1 Plato, writing in the fifth century BCE confirms this bilateral-influence: "there [are] as many types of character among men as there are forms of government . . . . constitutions [do not] spring from the proverbial oak or rock [but] from the characters of the citizens, which, as it were, by their momentum and weight in the scales draw other things after them" (*Republic* 544de).

the blood from his veins and replaces it with ice water." Some people can perhaps successfully make that transition between a starkly instrumental public or vocational persona and a caring and noble private self, but it takes a skill that most of us lack to hold together a life of radically isolated parts that share no common moral thread. Most of us will simply cave in to the logic of the system. Jürgen Habermas confirms this to be our overwhelming tendency: advanced industrial societies, he argues, colonize and deform communal life.[1]

Jacques Rancière posits a bulwark against industrialization's isolating and alienating effects. He cites a new globalizing middle class "sociality" of satisfied consumers who find solidarity in an "equality of condition" characterized by the "free exchange of goods, bodies, and candidates."[2] As local cultural and religious specificity falls away before a globalizing McWorld, Rancière reports that "commercial competition, sexual permissiveness, world music, and cheap charter flights to the Antipodes quite naturally create individuals smitten with equality and tolerance of difference?[3] Rancière's descriptions highlight the impoverished nature of the emergent global consumer culture. People may be growing increasingly identical, but clearly this new sociality can hardly be said to compose "community" in any sense that we intuitively recognize *as human*.

Simple Communal Societies

Industrialized consumer society leaves much to be *humanly* desired, but it is not the only form of community on the human map. Bartos posits a second form, a society that we might find in rural villages, isolated tribal settlements, or island communities.[4] Bartos calls this society "pre-industrial" and "traditional." I prefer to use "simple communal society" to avoid granting to industrialism and consumerism a sense of inevitability. This second form of society, at the far end of the politico-social spectrum

1 Jürgen Habermas, *The Philosophical Discourse of Modernity: Twelve Lectures* (Studies in Contemporary German Social Thought), Frederick G. Lawrence, trans. (Cambridge, Mass.: MIT Press, 1990).
2 Jacques Rancière, *Disagreement: Politics and Philosophy*, Julie Rose, trans. (Minneapolis: University of Minnesota Press, 1999), p. 20.
3 Ibid. p. 23.
4 Bartos and Weir, *Using Conflict Theory*, pp. 35, 44 ff.

from our own, may not exist anywhere in any pure form any more than industrialized consumer societies are purely dehumanizing and altogether degraded by materialism and the forces of late capitalism. Let us think of these two types of societies as extremes on a spectrum of possible politico-social forms, and that wandering-wondering along that continuum may prove to be a worthwhile exercise for reconsidering the options open to us for human dwelling.

Simple societies, tells Bartos, are characterized by horizontal differentiation, and suffer very little hierarchy. These communities enjoy internal structural advantages that have been developed over many generations, precisely to avoid the shortfalls of hierarchy. Complex systems of checks and balances minimize concentrations of power. Elaborate and highly nuanced traditions of social rituals monitor and direct social interactions. Face to face communication among its elements and highly complex mediation and resolution strategies reduce the chances and thus the frequency of social conflict. Family councils and committees of elders intercede and arbitrate in disputes, drawing in as many other members of the community as are required to increase the support base for both parties, and to creatively broaden the spectrum of options available for resolving conflicts.

What is crucial in communal societies is that the conflict ends in a win/win solution, where all parties are satisfied with the outcome. Since social unrest is understood and treated along the model of communal disease, the happiness of each individual and societal health as a whole become matters of extreme interest to all community members and a responsibility shared among them all. These small communities tend to be led by a council of elders or a single member of the community attributed with exceptional qualities. Where a single leader governs, she will have extraordinary charisma and reputation. She may be accorded special status for bravery in times of external threat, or skill in persuading others to a common goal or in negotiating among troubled parties. The leader may be chosen by hereditary right, through a link with some great tribal ancestor, or selected by a council of elders according to the timeworn customs of the community. But, in every case, the leader's legitimacy to govern is measured by the degree of social harmony that maintains under her direction, and by her conformity to traditional custom.

Just as the industrial society nurtures certain shared char-acteristics in its members and causes them to mirror the logic of their system, so too does the non-industrial model promote certain attributes and values emblematic of the system. People in these small societies are affective, emotively-connected, tend to like each other and mirror each other's values, and are prone to freely engage in frequent and gratifying interaction. They are far more communally oriented than industrial societies, broad-thinking and broad-skilled, less specialized in their vocations, tending rather toward skill-diffusiveness.

However, their highly communal nature does not mean that they fail to appreciate individuality. Indeed, as is indicated by the Swahili maxim *Mtu ni watu* ("person is people"), small soci-eties celebrate the community's ability to provide a stimulating setting for the budding of individual greatness. Remarkable in-dividuals arise within their social contexts. Because the small non-industrial society nurtures free interaction among its mem-bers, and because the members call upon each other freely to resolve their daily disputes and coalesce effectively to face chal-lenges threatening their group, there exists a high appreciation of individuals as crucial components of the whole, who bring special gifts to benefit the communal enterprise and unique tal-ents to serve during crises. Thus, these small societies tend to be both collectivistic *and* particularistic.

The Models Bleed Together

Having seen how the industrial society compares in char-acter with the non-industrial, obvious benefits suggest the de-sirability of transferring the social skill-sets, governance forms, conflict-management rituals, and value systems of the second simple type of community to the first industrial community. But this is no easy task. This simple society, just as Socrates' simple "city of pigs" (*Republic* 2.372a-d), though not an impossible ideal, represents a dying reality, as globalization sweeps the globe and middle class consumer sociality erodes local identity.

Furthermore, this simple model can only remain functional in small isolated groups, ideally 15 to 50 members, set apart a comfortable distance from their neighbors. Once a group exceeds fif-ty people, the ability of its members to interact in the face to face moral relations that promote peace and social harmony becomes severely reduced. The more dense the population, the less likely people will get along. As one colleague explained to me in my early shell-shocked days fighting traffic on Long Island freeways during my tenure at Adelphi University: "We are like rats in a box, Wendy; where we are only a few, we will share the cheese; where we are too many, we eat each other!"

Bartos explains the problem this way: groups must interact freely if they are to discover and cultivate the similarities that cause them to like each other. When they get to know and like each other and appreciate what they share in common, they gain a sense of community, and this shared sense of identity in turn causes them to seek out continued opportunities for free inter-action. They develop and share a common view of the world and agree upon its moral parameters. "This point is crucial," states Bartos, "[worldviews] cannot be imposed; they must evolve free-ly out of the opinions of individual members".[1]

So it seems quite impossible that our fevered and swollen consumerist societies might apply the positive features of these simple communities to our own systems and lives. However, there exist many sites of identity formation where people meet in groups of 15 to 50 to accomplish certain tasks—families, class-rooms, workplaces, church groups, town meetings, PTAs. In an alienating society, people seek out such community-building opportunities. This suggests the possibility and value of the de-velopment at these sites of social rituals promoting collectivistic values and conflict transformation skills. However, two prob-lems challenge a groups' successful internalization of positive collectivist traits and values.

First, when societies splinter into separate groups, individu-als seldom interact across their group's boundaries. Groups tend to become as isolated and alienated as individuals and then too relate to other groups in the manner of "zero sum games." Sec-ond and most important, when small groups interact freely, they not only build similarities that cause them increasingly to like

---

1 Bartos, Wehr, 2002, p. 75.

each other and to seek out further opportunities for free inter-action; the group solidarity that is a crucial condition for their self-identity is also a crucial condition for xenophobia. People in small groups appreciate each other for what they have in common, and their consciousness of their similarities quickly brings into relief the differences of others, whom they recog-nize as bereft of the qualities they appreciate in themselves and their friends. The solidarity of small communities soon gives rise to conflict ideology, as outsiders are seen as different to their good qualities, alien, threatening—evil. Conflict theory tells us that group solidarity and conflict ideology require but a trigger event to turn their group love into counter-group revulsion, then dread, and then aggression.

Counter-cultural rejection is a common phenomenon in groups of all shapes and sizes. A wealth of anthropological theo-ry confirms the tendency of human groups to gather in solidarity only through ritual acts of exclusion. In the worst cases, rituals of exclusion culminate in sacrificial violence. An internal inas-similable individual or an external enemy provides a crucial ser-vice to a community of any size; outsiders grant the occasion for group identity to solidify, by contrast to outgroup differences. René Girard claims univocally:

> All the great institutions of mankind, both secular and religious, spring from [the sacrifice] ritual. Such is the case . . . with political power, legal institutions, medicine, the theater, philosophy and anthropology it-self. It could hardly be otherwise, for the working base of human thought, the process of "symbolization," is rooted in the surrogate victim.[1]

The anthropological consensus is bleak: *Homo familias* and *Homo politicus* are also *Homo necans*.

Thus we may wish that small non-industrial societies would share with us their healthier worldview, social rituals, and com-munity-nurturing practices, but it is far more realistic to expect that, as globalization moves in to threaten traditional societies, collectivist values will give way to the industrial, market-driven

---

1 Girard, *Violence and the Sacred*, p. 306.

model. Will Rancière's middle class consumer sociality erase other alternative lifestyles? Can its shared condition offer some impoverished sense of community within the alienating industrial jungle of the globalizing McWorld? Will its fevered and swollen materialist sociality bring the troubling flux of social division to the stable shores of solidarity under a global politics of consumption?

The fact is that Rancière is mistaken: industrial society's middle class is not swelling any longer, but shrinking every year. A growing gap cleaves between global have's and have-not's, as in the industrialized West each year more people fall out of work and below the poverty line, while in the developing world, workers "race to the bottom" in ever-increasing competition for low-paying jobs. The swelling sociality is not the materialist have's (the well-meaned *euporai*) but the materially forgotten (the *aporoi*).

Far from global solidarity, the world is split in two. The elites of the West and comprador classes of developing nations cling together to maintain their global grip on planetary resources and cheap labor supplies, while the swelling poor, left to rot at the base of prosperity's ladder, cling ever more fervently to the opiates at their disposal—religious fanaticism and terrorist ideology. Conflict theory is clear: we will give them their due through democratic process or they will take it by bloody revolution. Their voices will be heard. Rancière states:

> There is nothing for it; there will always be surplus words, just as there are always fields abutting the ramparts or a mob pressing around the *ecclesia*. The many, in whatever form they appear, will continue to hold sway. No matter how many words are taken away, one can never silence the cries that stir up the crowd.[1]

Despite the tens of thousands of simple villagers who die each day from a lack of the necessities of life, the crowd of rabble at the global city's gates still swells and rattles louder, crying for their fair share of the common good, their crack at the "good and noble life" that they know in their human bellies should char-

---

1 Ibid. p. 30.

acterize every just society. In tyranny, the poor can simply be tortured, executed, or banished. But what will silence the cries of the poor, where the global ship of state can no longer send in the CIA to throw overboard the impoverished masses when they grow mutinous and demanding?

Conflict theory gives us much to think about in comparing our sickened societies to simpler, healthier ones, and its top-down coercive view of power affirms what we see before our eyes in our societies and across the globe. But I worry that Conflict Theory itself may inadvertently promote violent responses, since it rests upon certain unaddressed but dangerous assumptions. Conflict Theory suggests that human nature is such that conflict is inevitable, that the "war of all against all" is the natural state of human relations. Elites suppress their subordinates to maintain hegemony; the oppressed ultimately turn to revolutionary violence to overturn the system that oppresses them. Power really works like that, but it doesn't *only* work like that. The flaw in Conflict Theory is that it fails to acknowledge that power, as influence over others, works in all directions, not merely top-down and coercive. The human world is far more complex than Conflict Theory allows.

I don't know if human nature exists; and if it does, if it is primarily self-seeking and aggressive. I don't know if states are out to maximize their power at the expense of other states. I do know, as a violence scholar, that if we believe these theories and expect the worst of people, that we ourselves become more violence-prone. If we believe dark assumptions about our neighbors, we run the risk of becoming what we expect to find in them. We are changed by what we believe and our denigrating prophesies tend to recoil upon us and become realized in ourselves, as we arm ourselves to face a world we perceive as violent and threatening.

I don't know about human nature, but I know that nurture is a powerful force. A wife often shares the worldview of the husband who bullies her and actively supports him in his abuse; children take up the cruel practices of the authoritarian parent and revisit them on their own kids; groups tend to sink to the moral level of the worst of their members; victims cling to the categories invented to oppress them and become fanatical evangelists of the religions imposed upon them. Human beings are creatures of habit, and the habits we adopt are those of the powerful. Nurture is a powerful force and it does seep into our natures.

People tend to do what they have always done, and conflict is something that we have always done. But it doesn't have to be that way. Conflict Theory teaches us that conflicts can be resolved in various ways; the powerful may choose the ways of dictatorship or the ways of mediation. The powerless may take the road of democratic lobbying or may turn to radical violence. We can choose to meet the growing throngs of the world's poor with tear gas and fire hoses and guns. Or we can choose to meet their needs before their simple peaceful communities grow more desperate and violent. Many NGOs, like Global Exchange, offers us an alternative model for global relations, beyond the dehumanizing, profit-seeking, consumerist model of industrial community, a model for global relations that helps small peaceful communities to survive the onslaught of global capitalism with their families, their lifestyles, their value systems, and their dignity intact. Elite Globalization is opposed to Peoples' Globalization.

In today's world economy, where profit rules and small-scale producers are often left without resources or hope for their future, the Fair Trade movement rescues exploited producers from the cycle of hopelessness, poverty, and exclusion in which they have been historically trapped. The Fair Trade movement benefits almost a million farmers the world over, helping them to organize into cooperatives, form unions, seek micro-loans, network with others across the globe to provide for their families' basic needs and develop their communities; however, there is still much to be done. The Fair Trade movement has been successful in only forty-eight countries, and even there, farmers must still sell most of their crop outside of the Fair Trade system, because not enough companies are buying at Fair Trade prices, ultimately because the consumer does not vote for global justice with her dollar.

To those of us who can afford choices, it increasingly seems that global economic forces erode our capacity to help the less fortunate of the human family. But we do have a choice how our world proceeds from the current impasse. We can become more like the communal peoples, supporting our neighbors and resolving disparities (which will also help stop the flow of our jobs to impoverished areas overseas) or they will become more like us, greedy, selfish, aggressively self-promoting, and violent. Many activists who work to bring attention to the problem point toward love as the answer to the crisis. We shall consider in the coming chapters whether love is the solution or the cause of the problem.

CHAPTER NINE. THE SHAME OF HOMELY VIOLENCE

Some degree of conflict is inevitable at every level of identity—in homes, in churches, in schools, in sports leagues, in societies, and in the world, because in every group, no matter how deeply bonded the members, there exist vast human differences beyond the recognized similarities that grant their sense of community. Thus the terms of commonality, the "identity markers" of the group, will constantly come into view as inadequate, and will regularly have to be negotiated and renegotiated afresh. Indeed, though we share an undeniable sense of common character with our intimates, and a sense of being markedly different from outsiders, the truth is that there exist more differences *within* a single human group than between any two groups.[1] Because people are different from each other, differences of opinions and interests are continually emergent and ongoing and local definitions of commonality are always undergoing reconstruction.

Whenever a rich array of differences gathers in close proximity, we may expect those differences to regularly conflict with one another. Conflict, objectively considered, is simply a name we give to the condition of differences bumping up against one another. This condition of conflicted differences is inevitable at

1 Joseph L. Graves, Jr., *The Race Myth: Why We Pretend Race Exists in America* (New York: Penguin, 2005), p. 16.

every site of human dwelling where common identity is being carved out, but it occurs most frequently and is invested with exaggerated importance in the highly intimate dwelling place of the family home, where much is felt to be at stake in maintaining solidarity and unity at the same time that radical proximity brings into relief the inexorable individual differences. To say that conflict is an inevitable visitor at the home site is not to say that violence is inevitable as well. Violence is simply the least intelligent, least creative, least skillful or judicious response to the conflict situation, which is inevitable in every site of human dwelling.

Beyond the mere fact of the close intimacy of the family home, which brings difference into greater, and often exaggerated, relief, there are a number of features about the family home that leave it vulnerable to conflict, and therefore vulnerable to violence among unskilled navigators of human difference. Homely violence is promoted by the fact that a family is a system, an ordered ranking system, however benignly so. Inequalities and competitive pressures inhere in all ordered ranking systems. Homes are ordered in such a way that they elevate some members into a sense of entitlement and subordinate others to resentment and frustration. Both of these positions, entitled and disempowered, may purchase a sense of entitlement to use violence to promote one's own interests.

The institutionalized inequalities (political, economic and social), which are intrinsic to all systems, cultivate feelings of frustration and impotence at every level of social functioning, and they can elicit "ordering violence" from those in positions of authority, and violent reactionary responses from less powerful individuals and groups. Just as violence rebounds from adults to children and to the family dog, so in repressive systems the more powerful release their frustrations on the less powerful, and so on down the power chain. Ordered systems seem prone to adopt the operating logic that any amount of power, however limited, gives license to violate others less powerful. Hierarchies weigh heavily from the top down, and those on the bottom of the social ladder get the worst of it, being seen as fair targets for the frustrations of their many social superiors. Systems are nested within larger systems. Families are the smallest unit of the society, at the bottom of the network ladder, so it is hardly surprising that violence follows people home from the workplaces, the unemployment offices, and the traffic jams, to be visited upon intimates.

Industrialized societies are hierarchically ordered, so tend to be more violence prone than the simpler, more communal, cooperative social forms. However, we have seen in the previous chapter that the healthier communal societies are fast disappearing from the globe, as the competitive pressures of global capitalism pit worker against worker for diminishing employment opportunities, and as dwindling resources drive peoples' existential focus farther down Maslow's hierarchy, leaving them battling on the bottommost rungs of the need chain for the basic needs of life (food, shelter, physical security).

Even where homes cling obstinately to the gentler pole of the continuum of social forms, we may expect the current economic down-turn, which many experts predict to endure for the foreseeable future, to drive the most cooperative human communities toward frustrations and resentments, that will, if history repeats itself with any degree of consistency, find ultimate expression in increased incidence of violence, with its greatest release at the bottom of the power chain, in intimate violence within the poorest families.

We know for certain that social and economic pressures fuel violence at every level of society, which funnels down in turn into the family home. However, as sociologist William Stacey reminds us, "social forces do not batter women and children; conscious, free, responsible men do."[1] Research shows that batterers know full well what they do and can learn to overcome their violent behaviors, if they are determined to do so and they seek help. But do the men who are bullying and battering their wives and children really want to overcome their violent urges?

Many experts believe that batterers batter simply because they know they can get away with it; they know their victims to be powerless to stop them and it feels good to express their power over others. Like Bloch's Orokaiva pig hunters, battering partners resort to violent overflow onto those closest to them to

---

1 William Stacey and Anson Shupe, *The Family Secret* (Boston: Beacon Press, 1983), p. 24.

the highest degree of aggression that they feel certain of getting away with, reprisal-free. In counseling, I have on a number of occasions worked with people I categorize as "crisis junkies," for whom abusive or violent outbursts have an addictive quality linked to a pleasurable release that seems very like sexual orgasm.

Roy Baumeister, in his compelling study of human violence, *Evil: Inside Human Violence and Cruelty*, is in agreement with this explanation of perpetrator motivation—they do it because they can—arguing that cruelty and aggression are not a function of insecurity, low self-esteem, or self-loathing, but quite the opposite. People hurt people because of high self-esteem and blind, cruel arrogance. He states:

> There is ample reason to question whether low self-esteem is to blame for violence. Think of the obnoxious, hostile or bullying people you have known—were they humble, modest and self-effacing? (That's mainly what low self-esteem looks like.) Most of the aggressive people I have known were the opposite: conceited, arrogant, and often consumed with thoughts about how they were superior to everybody else. If one looks away from one's own acquaintances to the world's most notoriously violent criminals, the same pattern can be seen. When embarking on their aggressive campaigns, Saddam Hussein and Adolf Hitler were enormously confident and arrogant, adored by millions of followers. Indeed the Nazi claim to be the "Master Race" suggests that they believed in their collective superiority, not inferiority. Idi Amin was hardly a shy or humble person. Stalin and Mao had high opinions of themselves. One can easily go on listing such cases. Meanwhile, it is hard to find contrary examples.[1]

Baumeister's argument is compelling, but it rests on the assumption that low self-esteem always presents as humility, modesty, and self-effacement. This is simply not the case. Batterers can be much more complex people than this explanation allows.

---

1 Roy F. Baumeister, *Evil: Inside Human Violence and Cruelty* (New York: Freeman & Co., 1997), p. 136.

Explaining aggressive and bullying behavior as occurring simply because the aggressor knows he can or because bullying grants him a dizzying, gratifying sense of his own power seems to flagrantly beg the question: why does the bully, if he is so self-certain, so desperately *need* confirmation of his power that he engages in overt displays of brute force that place at risk his moral force? Baumeister might answer that the brute is so sure of himself that his actions never come into moral question for him; he cannot see that his actions are wrong. This argument would tempt agreement were it not for a common trait that links intimate abusers: they tend overwhelmingly and from early on in the relationship to isolate their victims and cut them off from external support systems (family and friends) that might open the intimate situation and their abusive behavior to public censure.

Moreover, we have plenty of evidence of truly great people, from the Dalai Lama to Mother Teresa, whose strong self of self-worth is expressed as humility and kindness. Perhaps having nothing to prove opens the space for a deep compassion for others, even for those others who fail them. I argue against Baumeister that beneath the aggressive self-assertion of the swaggering bully there is the sadness and frustration of a very unhappy person, suffering from various forms of cruel histories, unfortunate memories, and insecurities. Harming others is a very effective way to distract from one's own feelings of inadequacy, frustration, and deep sadness.

Let us take a few more examples. Hitler was a short, dark, ugly man, son of a bastard father, through whom, according to recent scholarship, he inherits Jewish and African blood.[1] Hitler was Austrian, only gaining German citizenship in 1932. He was not in any remote respect like the blonde, blue-eyed Aryan masculine ideal that he worshipped and promoted as the sole pure German identity. It is not a great psychological mystery that

---

1   Articles   in   *Huffington   Post*   (http://www.huffingtonpost. com/2010/08/25/hitler-jewish-dna-tests-s_n_693568.html)   *Knack* (Belgium)   http://www.knack.be/nieuws/wetenschap/hitler-was-verwant-met-somaliers-berbers-en-joden/article-1194797075630.html , and *The Daily Telegraph* (U.K.) http://www.telegraph.co.uk/history/ world-war-two/7961211/Hitler-had-Jewish-and-African-roots-DNA-tests-show.html argue that DNA evidence shows Hitler to have had Jewish and African blood. (All articles retrieved March 14, 2013)

Hitler was riveted to questions of legitimate German identity. Moreover, throughout his youth, Hitler had always dreamed of becoming an artist, but his applications to the Vienna Academy of Art, in 1907 and again in 1908, were both summarily denied. One might easily imagine Hitler to be the archetype of a man who needed desperately to confirm his identity and worth.

Similarly, Idi Amin was a man who might be expected to have severe identity crisis issues. According to a Special Report in the *Daily Monitor*, "Rejected then taken in by dad: a timeline," Fred Guweddeko tells that Amin's parents were separated in 1931 as a result of suspicion that the baby (Idi Amin) had been fathered by a lover.[1] Amin's father, Dada, rejected him, so he was forced to grow up with his maternal family and only three decades later, in 1964, did his father accept him back into his tribe. Idi Amin's early education amounted to rearing goats and reciting the Koran. He gained no more than a fourth grade English-language education and often worked demeaning service jobs until he was recruited into the British colonial army, where he served at Magamaga Barracks in Jinja as laundry and kitchen staff, until he transferred to Kenya for real military service.

Another life story of a brutal dictator tells a similarly sad story. Joseph Stalin was the son of a poor cobbler from Georgia. His smallpox-scarred face, his misshapen left arm, and his impediments with the Russian language (imposed upon him at the Georgian Orthodox Seminary from which he was ultimately expelled for missing his final exams and failing to pay his fees), offer themselves as ample proofs for deep-seated feelings of inadequacy that may have driven him to assert himself overzealously against others.

Psychologizing individual perpetrators is hardly a scientific way of determining the factors that motivate violence. However, life stories can be *humanly* compelling precisely because they resonate with our personal experiences and connect us sympathetically with people with whom we would otherwise feel no connection. We all know brutes whose mistreatment of others seems to baffle human understanding. But often when we learn

1 See http://web.archive.org/web/20070612053237/http://www.monitor.co.ug/specialincludes/ugprsd/amin/articles/index.php (retrieved March 14, 2013).

the details of the bully's life, a tale so *humanly* true unfolds that we begin to understand how a person's view of the world could become so skewed as to drive him to desperate measures.

The fact that Baumeister and I can interpret the same individuals in such divergent ways proves the idleness of objective speculations about what motivates individual perpetrators. However, plentiful studies of perpetrators show that the perpetrators suffer extremely high (almost 90%) incidence of deep-seated psychological pathology.[1] Psychologists who treat those abusive people who hurt their loved ones confirm that the secrets to intimate abuse lie within the perpetrator psyche. They confirm that intimate perpetrators hurt others because they feel badly about themselves. Batterers feel inadequate, ashamed, and often enraged, and almost entirely these psychological traits are linked to their childhood experiences, which left deep psychological scars. In childhood abusive people were themselves repeatedly abused, beaten, humiliated, and made to feel powerless, helpless, and inadequate because of their inability to protect themselves and their intimate fellows from abuse.

Cruel treatment in childhood teaches the victims and the helpless bystanders that only the powerful survive. Thereby, power becomes a trumping good to gentleness and nonaggression in their developing inventory of values. When these childhood victims grow into adulthood and find themselves in situations of dominance, at the first signs that chaos is returning to their lives, they may rush to the big guns to quell the disorder. Moreover, even in less dire times, they may project their bad feelings onto their loved ones, choosing as targets for their frustrations those who cannot easily retaliate. Damaged people push other, weaker persons down to enjoy a sense of elevation, because elevation, however won, temporarily masks their shame and eclipses their sense of powerlessness.

In the 1960s, just as the magnitude of the problem of aggression in American society was entering the public consciousness, psychologist Rollo May shocked readers with his studies of violence that implicated both the victim and the perpetrator in explaining perpetration. May argued in his book *Power and Innocence*

---

1 Linda G. Mills, *Violent Partners*, pp. 92-106.

that powerlessness is not merely coincidental to the fact of victimization but innocence invites its own abuse. The invitation to abuse, contends May, is an irresistible incitement for feeble-ego'ed people who seek to overcome their low self-esteem.

Prominent among the palette of negative affects that perpetrators have gained from their histories of abuse is the destructive affect of shame. Shame is a powerful emotion that lodges deep down in a victim's core, undermines their sense of well-being, and drives them toward violence. Experts have charted the growing levels of violence in Western societies, even as those societies have grown more prosperous and provided more material ben

efits to their people. Yet few social analysts have made the shrewd connection that Michael Moore explores with the outrageous punk rocker Marilyn Manson in his documentary film about American violence, *Bowling for Columbine*. Manson makes the powerful charge that all those hours of media advertising, to which youngsters are exposed daily, leave them with feelings of inadequacy and shame. The consumer is told that she needs a special toothpaste to disguise her foul breath, and special deodorant to dispel the fetid stench of her body. Without Prada, and Saturn and Nike and Rolex, *people are branded* as less valuable human beings. And the thing about purchasing one's identity by owning things is that no amount of accumulated stuff is ever adequate to reach down to the deep angst of inadequacy. Whatever we have, we are a left hungering for more, and never released from our shame.

To my mind, negative affects underlie and drive perpetration. They assume many diverse forms, of lesser and more debilitating intensity and depths. Anger, fear, frustration, jealousy, and resentment exist closer to the surface, easily notable by those in proximity. More dangerous and more nebulous "bad me" feelings are concealed below conscious level. Deeper still, if we peel back the layers of existential angst, we find the deepest, most debilitating affect of all, shame. In the next chapter I will make the case that shame is the most dangerous of the negative affects that inhere in the depths of our being; it is hardest to identify (because its roots are so deep and because we hide it so well fro m ourselves) and hardest to dislodge (because its effects are not only empirical but ontological).

CHAPTER TEN. WHAT'S EROS GOT TO DO WITH IT?

We have seen that violent urges inhere in human nature, alongside dispositions to nurture and cooperate. We have seen too that these conflicting forces render environments the crucial site for shaping people's habits and behaviors and disposing people toward violence or compassion. We have also discovered that conflict is inevitable wherever human differences meet up with each other, and that in the home, as a particularly close meeting place, an exaggerated importance may be placed upon unity and solidarity, which can propel violence, as an unskilled conflict response style. Violence per se, in the sublimated form of structural oppression, will already likely inhere in the structure of the home, as an ordered institution that seeks integrity, coherence, and continuance, within the context of evolving differences.

Like other systems, the family's integrity, coherence, and continuance are fostered by shared beliefs (which can erode), shared interests (which can come into conflict), and shared goals (which can change over time). Like other systems, the family seeks stability over time through ordering rituals. Ordering rituals involve rankings, which by definition privilege some members and disadvantage others. Like other hierarchical systems, the family sorts out its members and keeps the balance of power and interests by ranking the members on a scale of importance, according to their relative fragility or their relative power. Because members command differing degrees of attention to their needs, enjoy differing seniority in the group, and have differing relations of power, the family systemic structure has a tendency to pit members against each other in what the conflict theorists name "zero sum" contests—where some members come out winners and others losers—and these contests tend to isolate individuals, fragment the group, and leave everyone resentful.

We have also discovered that family homes are shaped by the larger systems that contain them. Some societies, small communalistic societies, have shown themselves better equipped to cultivate cooperation among their citizens, since there is less competitivism, less hierarchy, elaborate timeworn ritual strategies of conflict management supported by cultural myth, and an ethos that supports individual distinction. We have seen that industrialized consumer societies, on the other hand, have a tendency to pit people against one another for jobs, power, and material resources. The entrepreneurial ethos, which claims that anyone can become rich if they simply work hard and apply themselves, may cultivate shame in society's poorer members by "branding" them as losers and blaming them for their poverty. We must not underestimate the effect of the society at large for shaping the ethos of the families it contains. Degraded ideas of human success, as measured by wealth, power, or fame, and callousness toward society's victims work together to provide a pitiful cradle for nurturing *human* values among the families that populate the society.

This wide array of structural reasons helps us to understand some of the external forces that may lead to unskilled—violent—responses to conflict situations when human differences arise in the family home. The weight of these external forces should not be undervalued. However, let us return to the question of internal forces that may be lying in wait to waylay our loving family. One critical feature that can motivate unskilled responses to the conflict situations that inevitable arise in the home is the very feature we may count on to hold the family in peaceful bonds. In this chapter, we shall take up just this question, asking with Tina Turner, that famed singer and survivor of intimate abuse, "What's love got to do with it?"

Some readers will object that our study thus far has not truly understood the phenomenon of home, in focusing upon the family as a system. The family is different from other institutions, they may argue. While it shares institutional structure, the glue that holds the structure intact is of a different kind. The glue that holds the homespace together is not desire for profit, ideological vision, or political agenda, nor even reproduction, fecundity, or genetic improvement of the clan. The glue that holds the structure intact, the adhesive force that turns a mere house into a home, is love.

Love, the defender of homespace will protest, is more binding than the beliefs, interests, and goals that unite other forms of institutional structures. Love causes the home to be greater than the sum of its parts, because its binding force is not shared interests but a shared ethic of selflessness. Love sets aside personal triumphs for the sake of the good of the beloved. The home has greater durability than other institutions because the love that binds it can endure the most challenging political, economic, and social upheavals and can shake free of the onerous weight of its structural form. Love is a good of the highest order: one that is good *in itself* as well as a good *for the sake of* other benefits that it brings. So the story goes, from the ancient poems and myths to the modern love song to Hollywood film.

It is precisely because we all hold so fast to these lofty tales about love that violence at the homespace is the baffling mystery that it is. Thus, if we are to understand the violence that is so frequently suffered and doled out at the homespace, we must glean a better—more realistic—understanding of love. We must identify the weaknesses and shortcomings that cause its effects to fall short of our tall expectations. We must locate the problematic aspects of love that frustrate the mutual support and understanding we expect it to nurture at the homespace. To locate love's dangers and pitfalls, we will turn to the many philosophers who have meditated upon the nature of love.

Love is a passion that, by its very nature, runs to the excess and overflows the banks of reason. Plato calls love, in all its many forms, a madness, though he qualifies it as a madness that is heaven sent (*Phaedrus* 244ab). In the *Symposium*, he has Socrates declare that love is the one thing about which he (Socrates, the know-nothing) knows the truth. Here, against the backdrop of legendary tales and eulogies to the god of love, offered by poet, orator, and comedian, Socrates reveals the truth: love is not a powerful god but a daemon, a needy waif of a half-god, incapable of the great feats of fulfillment we generally attribute to him.

We have seen in the opening chapters of this book that Plato has much to say about love. Plato's wide range of stories, recounted by the eulogists, the doctor, the tragic-comic poet, the priestess, and the know-nothing philosopher, and the tragic love tale demonstrated in the agonized flesh of the tormented Alkibiades express the complexity of this fundamental human emotion. Love is not only divine beauty and light, as the eulogists had it in their speeches, but it is also a lot of pain and confusion and moral degradation. There is a certain fateful playfulness encoded in Plato's myths about love whose tragic tenor cannot be shaken despite the laughable imagery of round little creatures rolling up to the heavens and drunken lovers, crowned in ivy and violets.[1]

We meet again this tragic, fateful playfulness in the love myths of the Hebrew Bible, in the tales of Adam and Eve in the Garden of Eden (Genesis 2 and 3), Ahab and Jezebel (1 Kings 16:31), and David and Bathsheba (2 Samuel, 11). From the philosophers to the Abrahamic holy books to the writings of the mystic and bard, the fateful playfulness of love is a dangerous *jouissance* that rarely turns out well for the lovers. Sometimes, the risk is one-sided, with one of the lovers paying a higher price than the other for their shared passionate indulgence. But more often than not, love is a just distributor of its insufferable fruits, doling out equal measures of its pleasures and pains to both parties, as with the star-crossed lovers Romeo and Juliet.

Often the joy comes first to lure the lovers into its lair, but invariably it is followed later by disillusionment and pain. The greater the heights of joy to which love initially leads the couple, the greater the depths of the pain and despair that they may expect when the desired blissful destiny fails to be realized. Hol-

---

1 Plato, *Symposium* 212d.

lywood makes a good profit by turning this chronology on its ear, turning initial pains into joyful endings. Love that succeeds sells tickets. Few movies are willing to risk the box office take by shattering the illusion that love can fulfill itself in mutual satisfaction.

The 1987 romantic comedy film "Moonstruck" is a typical romantic comedy that allows love to triumph in the end. What is rare in this film, directed by Norman Jewison, is that it brings about the desired happy ending through the argument that love is not about happy endings. In the climax of the film, the crippled but handsome young Italian baker, Ronny, tries to convince his brother's fiancée, Loretta, to leave a safe and predictable future with Johnny to follow him along the path of passion. Loretta resists believing the irrational choice will bring her to a bad fate, but Ronny, with arresting frankness, cries:

> Loretta, I love you. Not like they told you love is. Love don't make things nice; it ruins everything. It breaks your heart. It makes things a mess. We aren't here to make things perfect. The snowflakes are perfect. Not us! Not us!

Having destroyed Loretta's illusions about love as a prudent plan culminating in a sensible destiny, Ronny raises himself up like a Greek god, drunk in the garden, barefoot and pleading, and echoes the ugly truth about love that Plato's myth had intimated: *We are here to ruin ourselves, to break our hearts, to love the wrong people, and die!*

This romantic comedy ends with everyone gathered around the family table, kibitzing and hugging and shouting and eating, and ultimately working things out to everyone's satisfaction. The ending mirrors a certain truth about family life that sends us home from the theater happy—families can endure a heck of a lot of deceit and betrayal and agony. But something about Ronny's agonized dialogue stays with us, and intimates a deeper truth than happy endings around the family table. While we all desire peace and stability in our lives, and trust that sensible, secure futures are hatched from well-laid rational plans, it is Plato's divine madness that we most desperately crave. We long to find ourselves caught up in a force greater than our prudent plans, something powerful and dangerous and crazy, that drags us away from the everyday, tears us, tortures us, perhaps ruins us, but even in the ruining, reminds us that we are alive and not merely breathing, not merely satisfying needs.

The love that is most coveted is the love that drives us to madness. We want desperately to interrupt our routine lives in the "shallow end" of human existence, where it is risk-free and pain-free, but monotonous and dreary. In *The Prophet*, Kahlil Gibran captures the distinction between love's dangerous passion and the passionless everydayness of daily life, in the counsel that Almustafa offers to the people of Orphalese on the subject of love:

> When love beckons to you follow him,
> Though his ways are hard and steep.
> And when his wings enfold you yield to him,
> Though the sword hidden among his pinions may wound you.
> And when he speaks to you believe in him,
> Though his voice may shatter your dreams as the north wind lays waste the garden.

The prophet warns not against ruin; he counsels embracing it, abandoning oneself to the devastation. Love's ruin is depicted as no less natural and elemental than the north wind, spiky-feathered wings, and rocky climes. The prophet warns against the cowardly prudence that would rob us of love's wounding reality. Almustafa declares:

> But if in your fear you would seek only love's peace and love's pleasure,
> Then it is better for you that you cover your nakedness and pass out of love's threshing-floor
> Into the seasonless world where you shall laugh, but not all of your laughter, and weep, but not all of your tears.

The longing for escape from the "seasonless world" of budgeting, grocery runs, and carpools explains why people keep coming back for more, even when love leaves them pierced and bleeding, ravages their peaceful existence, and wrecks their best-laid plans.

Psychoanalyst-philosopher Julia Kristeva analyzes the existential attraction that tempts people into love's territory. She tells, in *Tales of Love*: "Love is a time and a space within which 'I' assumes the right to be extraordinary . . . equal to the infinite space of superhuman psychisms. Paranoid? I am, in love, at the zenith of subjectivity."[1] Love opens the lovers to their superhuman aspect, enlarges the present of subjectivity beyond its normalized bounds. The subjective "present" of love is always bound up as well with promises and hopes and dreams, with a future; love projects the subject into the "future perfect" where they "will have been" happy someday. The longing, which is felt in the presence of the beloved, represents not only an enlargement of subjectivity, but a beyond of the self, an escape from the suffocating presence of subjectivity, with its duties and responsibilities and projects, its rules and conventions. Love is catharsis to the disciplines of routine, passion to the reasons of customs and habits and schedules—festival to the mundane.

Love is an emotive eruption within the mundane. Perhaps this fact holds the key to our understanding of the violence that so frequently configures intimate relations. The release that breaks the lovers free from the everyday also ruptures the bounds of propriety and decency that hold the civilized world intact. In ancient Athens, festival released wives and children from the enclosure of the household; it released slaves to the sovereignty of command; it released enthusiasts to their cults with their bloody, orgiastic rites—ritual madness, trances, strange prophecies, speaking in "tongues," torturous mutilations, dismembering animal (and occasionally human) victims, and eating the bodies. For a few short days, ancient festival elevated people from their mundane lives to the realm of the sacred, connecting them with the powerful energies of other spirit-worlds.

Ancient festival appeared to threaten to devastate the artifacts of civilization and scatter individual existences, but in reality, the festival's climax gathered the group together again into solidarity, confirming ordinary life. The very rites of dance and song, drink and drug, and rituals of murder and plunder that lifted the people into a shared experience of ecstasy and released their pent-up energies and frustrations, also confirmed the community's traditions and institutions, because the final episode of

---

1 Julia Kristeva, *Tales of Love*, Leon S. Roudiez, trans. (New York: Columbia University Press, 1987), p. 5.

the festival returned people to their mundane places and duties, refreshed, renewed, and unified. Slaves went back to the fields, wives to the kitchen, children to the nursery, and men to their duties in the *ekklesia*, the Areopagus, and the *agora*, satisfied once more with the conventional order of their world.

The modern fragmented world enjoys no more shared communal festivals. Isolated individuals are left to find, in any way they can, ecstatic release from the shallow concerns of their daily lives, growing shallower by the day under the influence of a globalizing industrial, bureaucratic capitalism. Love's passion is one of the few remaining escapes from the vapid barrenness of consumer culture. We seek an overwhelming experience of love to release us from our mindless addictions to the commodities and technologies that control our lives, our identities, and our destinies. Fools, we crave a blazing encounter with the daemonic wanderer, indigent, sleeping in doorways. Will the love we crave leave us ruined and homeless at the close of the festival, or will it bring us back to the family table, return us to the everyday rejuvenated and newly committed, and confirm and preserve the institutions that order our lives?

To consider whether love undermines or confirms family life, it may be helpful to consider the phenomenon of being "in love," to consider more closely the passions we associate with love, how love feels to the subject that is undergoing it, what emotions love elicits in its victims. The emotive symptoms of love include: trembling voice, parched throat, starry eyes, dizzy head, blurred vision, flushed or clammy skin, throbbing, racing heart, scattered thoughts, and befuddled mind. In love we are in the world in a wholly different emotive way, in the world but apart from the world, elevated by our stormy passions. Kristeva identifies the irony—and the danger—of love.[1] Are the symptoms of love not the very same symptoms we suffer in the face of impending danger? Are they not suspiciously akin to the symptoms of horror and fear?

If what we crave, in love, is the removal from the everyday, the state of elevation above normalcy, and if this elevated state shares symptoms with fear and horror, then the overlap of the

---

1 Ibid., p. 6.

symptoms of love with the symptoms of fear and horror may offer us a glimpse into the worldview of the woman who defies
reason, baffles her friends and counselors, and abandons her own
best interests by returning again and again to the homespace
where her abusive lover awaits her. Perhaps over the course of
a passionate relationship, the thrill of love's divine madness becomes so profoundly entangled with terror and pain that a victim loses her ability to distinguish between the two. She may
mistake her terror for a passion so lofty that well-meaning others cannot possibly understand it.

If love can be understood only through its festival quality, through emotional upheavals of the body and scattered
thoughts in the mind, the challenge for lovers will be to manage
their festivals, so that on the morning after, they may return to
their mundane lives, enriched and renewed, rather than banned
from their homes to a life of forbidden mysteries. Hollywood and
ancient Athens got it right: we need a happy ending if love is to
be declared the glue that holds the household intact and keeps
the wolf of violence at bay. But Plato warns succinctly in the
Phaedrus: Lovers love their loves as wolves love lambs. Will the psychoanalyst agree?

The psychoanalyst's prognosis for love is not favorable. In
her meditation upon the star-crossed lovers, Romeo and Juliet, Kristeva posits three alternative fates for lovers. None of
the three is anything akin to what we intuitively know as love.
None gives us the happy ending at the family table. Shakespeare
chooses the easy way out of love's three-horned dilemma. He
preserves the lovers' passion by killing them off before their love
wanes or sickens. Kristeva tells, Shakespeare "conforms to pro-
prieties for once; having them die, he saved the pure couple."[1]
Killing off the impassioned lovers saves them from the crueler
fates that the analyst predicts for married couples:

> Either time's alchemy transforms the criminal secret
> passion of the outlaw lovers into the banal, humdrum,
> lackluster lassitude of a tired and cynical collusion: that
> is normal marriage. Or else the married couple contin-
> ues to be a passionate couple, but covering the entire

1 Ibid.

gamut of sadomasochism . . . . Each acting out both sexes in turn they thus create a foursome that feeds on itself through repeated aggression and merging, castration and gratification, resurrection and death. And who, at passionate moments, have recourse to stimulants—temporary partners, sincerely loved but victims still, whom the monstrous couple grinds in its passion of faithfulness to itself, supporting itself by means of its unfaithfulness to others.[1]

Kristeva sees only three paths that the lovers can take: passionate death, death of passion, or the pathological love of sadomasochism. Each of the three paths is deeply tragic.

"Romeo and Juliet" is categorized in the genre of tragedy because it conforms to the tragic model: whatever the well-intended heroes do, in their efforts to elude their fate and bring about a happy ending for themselves, their choices are the very ones that bring about their cruel destiny. They lose the battle for (mere) life, but win the grander prize of glory—their place in the annals of heroic deeds, at which ordinary people always fail. Tragic lives are lives well lived but cut short, at the height of their triumph.

What is the great victory, the distinguishing feat, for which we continue to remember Romeo and Juliet? Their heroic accomplishment was a love that did not burn out or sour. It did not give in to adversity, though all the world was against them. Their unhappy ending—their death—was a happy ending for their love, immortalizing it.

Kristeva follows the lovers down the path not taken and reveals to us two alternative fates that wait at the end of the path of love, the marital path. Both are deeply tragic destinations, more heartrending than the fate Shakespeare chose for Romeo and Juliet. No place in the annals of heroic deeds will be reserved for the sufferers of these tragic ends, the lovers fated for marriage. Here the path splits again. To one side, the lovers find their way to a "tired and cynical collusion" that is "banal, humdrum, lackluster." Many will recognize the model. Passion is gone, but life drones on—mortgages, 401(k)s, PTA meetings, alcohol-

---

1 Ibid., p. 217.

sopped middle age, graying or balding hair, sexual dysfunction, perhaps affairs and sports cars to quench the regret, religion to soothe the shame, elaborate funeral plans to repair the record of bad plays. People often go to elaborate lengths to rewrite, repair, or mourn this commonplace tragedy.

To the other side of the marital path, Kristeva offers a second kind of marriage, distinguishable from the "normal" yet not named "abnormal" either. In this model, passion is kept alive by a cyclical pathology; the lovers take turns at suffering and torturing each other. In this scenario, love's addictive quality is fueled by intervals of withholding, followed by intense episodes of passionate renewal and commitment. Withheld love can be agonizing and crushing, but when the torture stops, the payoff arrives in emotional hard currency, cash payments of high dose endorphins. Crisis junkies, these couples enjoy little down time from the festival of love's passion, which alternates between its dark face and its fair. Too often physical cruelty joins the psychological abuse of withholding, to which both parties look for an outlet for their frustration. This kind of love is the hardest to escape, because as the cycles of cruelty spiral, so too does the emotional payoff of reconciliation. Few outside the relationship can understand why the two sickened lovers keep coming back for more. And they do tend to come back for more, an addiction so compelling that few besides alcoholics and drug addicts will understand the powerful temptation to self-destruction. But ultimately the two faces of love—sadistic and masochistic—bleed together, so that the doubt and pain suffered during withholding undermines the fundamental bond, and sours the erotic pleasure of making up.

A loveless cynicism or a passionate coupling that feeds on itself and others in cycles of aggression and submission: is Kristeva's dichotomy of marital tragedy exhaustive of love's possibilities? Must Eros be always entangled with Thanatos, as Kristeva declares, after Freud? Is there no love that doesn't sicken, collapse our well-being, murder our dreams, and tear at the fabric of family life and societal harmony? Kristeva, the analyst whose vocation exposes her to a constant stream of couples in crisis, holds out no such hope for the lovers. However, some alternative love *must* be found, if we are to rescue the home from the unruly passion that festers and flares into violence. We need a love that funnels and disciplines the chthonic energies into daily routines and duties and that grants meaningful interruptions in the hum-drum—birthday celebrations, Super Bowl parties, and holidays at the seaside—without dousing the flames of healthy desire, fueling the jealousies of differences, or purchasing the internal bond through murder of outsiders.

CHAPTER ELEVEN. WHAT'S SHAME GOT TO DO WITH IT?

From the inception of philosophy as a distinct practice and epistemological orientation, philosophers have explained the peculiarity of their art as the wisdom of unknowing. Pythagoras captures this meaning in his original naming of the art as *philossophos*, meant to distinguish philosophy from sagacity and the philosopher from the all-knowing sage. Love of wisdom or the desire for wisdom distinguishes the philosopher as the rare self-aware individual, who admits her emptiness of certain knowledge; always seeking but never reaching truth, the philosopher is very distinct from the sage, *sophos*, or the arrogant teacher, the sophist, in the practice of her art and in her humble orientation toward the truth. We witnessed this humble unknowing in Socrates, who places his certain knowledge about love in the mouth of the Manitean priestess. The Buddha expresses the same ethos of humility in his dictum to his followers: "If you meet the Buddha on the path, slay him."

Contra the general prejudice against philosophers as useless dreamers of abstract ideas, disconnected from empirical realities, philosophers have traditionally concentrated their energies precisely on practical matters. The best philosophers have kept their focus riveted on "the right conduct of life." Right conduct refers to the clarification of values, the identification of virtues that serve those values, and the development of the art of statesmanship which might bring societies to a state of justice, as balanced, harmonious coexistence. The point is not to simply increase our knowledge; knowledge is the domain of the sophist. The philosopher is more interested in *how we live* and how the state can shape people for harmonious dwelling than *what we know.*

When we do our best work in the world—as philosophers, parents, teachers, and citizens—it is not usually as know-it-all heroic adventurers, accurately pre-calculating the ethical profits and losses of our actions. Rather, when families, school rooms, and societies run smoothly and leave people feeling safe and happy, it is often because of the uncalculated labors of many responsible persons, whose efforts are often torn from them, rather than freely given. We pay our taxes because we must. We tend our sick child, despite our own intense need for sleep. We stay after class to help a struggling student, though we prefer to go home to our families. Good acts are rarely simple acts of good intention and even our best works are less than purely good; every act is morally ambiguous, as its effects tumble down the infinite path of their futures, betraying the interests of others who lie outside our knowledge and our circle of responsibility.

Postmodern philosophers have tried to capture the elusive contradictions of moral choice, by citing guilt and mourning as the rubric affects under which all moral acts are undertaken. For Emmanuel Levinas, the moral affect *par excellence* is guilt; we feel ashamed for our incapacity to help *all* our neighbors, our inability to feed *all* widows, orphans, and aliens, and our failure to adequately hostage ourselves to every suffering person's needs. We are often too late and too powerless to insert ourselves responsibly into situations of other people's irresponsibility. Even those with the most willing hearts and the fullest hands are unsure how to best proceed and their hesitation brings them too late to the crisis, helpless to spare the next victims.

For Jacques Derrida, the moral rubric is mourning; we feel shame for the harm that our decisions will cause beyond the scope of our control and ken. We cannot, in good conscience, simply succumb to the temptation to endlessly delay our response to the needy, as did the allies during World War Two or the United Nations during the Rwandan Genocide. We *must* act, to be morally fit human beings, and we *must* act right away, to minimize the harm that is always already going on in so many areas of the world and in our own lives. Whatever we do, we remain guilty for what we cannot do and for the unforeseen ill effects of those very things we have done to try to help.

Guilt and mourning are cited, by these, and many other, postmodern philosophers, as the emotive tools for enacting our ethical work in the world. Shame has long been employed in Western societies as tool for ethical conditioning. Since the ancient Greeks, military and aristocratic societies have employed shame as a useful moral teacher, shaming the cowards who flee the battlefield, while honoring those who are valiant warriors. Philosophers of the ancient world hold shame in high regard, as the voice of a healthy conscience. Socrates is ashamed to sneak out of the prison, even to save his life; he freely accepts the hemlock rather than shame himself by fleeing and breaking his city's laws. Shame is fundamental to the humility ethos of the philosopher, as well as to the honor code of the warrior. Shame undersits as well the Talmudic tradition of aporetic hermeneutics. From the Greeks and the Jews, the tradition finds its way into Christianity as well, in the asceticism of priests (against which Nietzsche's Zarathustra rails), and in the shame that gathers around sex and the bodily functions. There is little innovation in the postmodern ethics that calls upon shame as a useful pedagogical tool for instilling prohibitions and cultivating the desired virtues.

However, there is little doubt that shame and its aspects of guilt and mourning, are negative affects, destructive emotions that can cripple our hearts and leave us paralyzed toward our own and others' sufferings. It is therefore crucial that we understand whether shame can also have the positive effects on our moral bearing that the philosophers claim it can have. Let us be certain that this pedagogical tool is the best that ethics can use, before applying it to teach moral behavior in our already violence-prone homes.

Shame is a sting felt in the depth of the soul that is painful and humiliating. The pain and humiliation alert the subject to her moral failure. Anthropologists of violence assure us that the lessons learned in pain are the lessons most deeply learned, and shame is a particularly effective form of pain that works through the emotions to teach people very deeply. Walter Burkert tells: Special forms of learning are made indelible 'at a stroke,' without repetition. . . . Every individual will have unforgettable memories of this kind, especially of a painful or humiliating character. [This learning is called] "anxiety learning."[1]

We feel ashamed for a moral fault that offends our sense of what we *ought* to be doing, that contradicts our society's shared codes of moral duty. We can also feel shame for the moral faults of our children, since we accept as an aspect of our moral duty the moral teaching of our children. Because we know what we ought or ought not be doing, we enjoy the benefit of shame's moral alert. Shame sounds the warning bell, stops us in our tracks, interrupts and paralyzes our spontaneous freedom. Shame warns before we slip off the moral cliff. Then, if we continue on our deliberative course despite shame's warning, we will experience the even greater pain and humiliation of the fall from the grace of our community.

However, there is a fundamental flaw in this debilitating affect: shame rests on a moral paradox. Shame is an affective response which brings to attention an impending ethical failure, which recognition is only possible where there has preceded an epistemological success. We can only feel guilty for moral failure, where we have achieved adequate moral learning. We can measure how far we have morally fallen, precisely because we have knowledge of the boundaries that we should never cross, the borderlines of prevailing mores. Shame cannot be much of a pedagogical tool if it only teaches those who don't need teaching.

But this pedagogical failure in a tool designed expressly for pedagogical success in moral matters is the least of shame's shameless failings. Since shame can only occur where moral lessons have already been learned, the morally ignorant are incapable of shame and its benefit warnings. A good example of this

1 Walter Burkert, *The Creation of the Sacred*, pp. 30 & ff.

comes to us in Plato's *Gorgias*, when the young fool Polus, student of the famed orator Gorgias, declares a shameful opinion: that anyone should feel jealous of the fortunate tyrant who can get away with "killing or imprisoning or depriving [others] of property" (*Gorg.* 468e).

Polus is shaming himself with this blatant celebration of injustice, yet he does not *know* enough to feel ashamed. He is epistemologically challenged, which has dire moral consequences for his personal moral code and also speaks to his potential behaviors. He has not completed his moral lessons to the point where shame can function to stop him short, before his shameless words have been spoken. Polus is shaming himself, but he does not *know* that he is. Shame is an affect that has no effect on those who most need it. Shame fails to teach Polus, who is desperate for its lessons, whereas it is working overtime on affecting everyone else present. The moral fall-out of Polus' shameless speaking extends across the city of Athens. First, Polus is shaming his teacher Gorgias, who is standing by, watching him (Polus) speak so imprudently. Polus' shameless speech evidences the problem with his teacher's professional ethic, a problem that Socrates, only moments before, had been illuminating before the crowd. Gorgias does not take responsibility for his students who go morally astray. Gorgias is made to see, in the example of his shameless students, the problem with a pedagogy that takes no responsibility for its failure to teach. Gorgias has had adequate moral training to recognize the problem. This learning is evidenced in his response to Socrates' exposure of the shortcomings of his art: Gorgias felt ashamed.

Polus has not had the benefit of the moral training that Gorgias, his teacher, evidences. He is incapable of feeling ashamed of his scandalous words. Gorgias is ashamed *for him*, as is Socrates. Polus' shameful speech is shaming Socrates, because it was his (Socrates') argument that elicited and exposed in the public space this most unsightly speech, a speech that, once let out of the bag, is not easily put back in, without leaving its dangerous traces in the many minds gathered at this meeting. Indeed if we accept Socrates' argument to his accusers in the *Apology*, Polus' shameless speech is shaming all the citizens of Athens, since it is everyone's duty to take aside the unlearned and teach them the moral lessons they have missed.[1] Everyone here is guilty, yet the pedagogical tool of shame has done no real work. The shame that attaches to Polus' act (of speaking imprudently) fails to do any moral labor in this moral moment; it fails to stop short Polus' tongue. The moral paradox of shame is that it only teaches those who have already learned their moral lessons. It has no pedagogical power to alter the behavior of those who most need its lessons. Shame, like Gorgias, fails to teach those it promises to teach, fails to stop the potentially morally faltering from actual moral failure.

Shame is used broadly across our societies, from the nursery to the schoolroom, to the churches, and into the houses of parliament and the oval offices. Shame is instilled in the soul of the learner by society in general, and it is used by teachers, priests, judges, and parents to teach their moral lessons. It is broadly used because it is useful. When shame sounds its warning bell and saves the moral agent before she goes tumbling over the cliff of foul deeds, it proves itself to be a most helpful tool. If shame would only show up on time, it could save us much heartache, and shore up our store of moral confidence.

However, the fact is shame doesn't usually show up in time. Even to the morally learned and eager, who intend to do good at every opportunity and to avert harm doing at all costs, shame is an unskilled messenger of impending moral doom; its alert all too often fails to arrive in time to save us from our pain and humiliation. Sometimes, it fails to show up at all, because our moral error lies beyond our limited human foresight. At other times, shame teaches us very unhelpful lessons that can undermine our moral confidence altogether: it teaches us all too clearly that people cannot control the infinite effects of their actions, even when their intentions are pure. All the moral learning in the world cannot save us from the pain and humiliation of shame, when shame has failed us—failed to show up in time to avert the catastrophe and save our moral face. It seems we are Epimetheus' offspring, seeing things clearly only in hindsight, doomed to learn, when we learn at all, through looking backward over our mistakes.

---

1 Plato, *Apology* 26a.

Putting aside the many problems of shame's frequent malfunctioning, let us consider how well shame does work, when it functions as it is intended. Shame is an affective confirmation of a transgression. But that affect carries *ontological* consequences. *What I have done* has implications for *who I am*, both in my self-estimation and in the estimation of my community, where the moral rules originate. If I have *done* wrongly, I *am* shameful. Shame works by placing a painful and humiliating burden upon the bearer, inciting in her deep self-doubt about her moral worth. Shame's burden is so weighty that it can cripple the bearer, and disfigure her fragile, breath-like soul. Under the crippling weight of shame, we become like the monster sea-god Glaucus, whom Socrates describes in the *Republic* as a creature whose first nature can hardly be made out by those who catch a glimpse of him, because the original members of his body are broken off and mutilated and crushed, and in every way marred by the waves [so that] he is more like some wild creature than what he was by nature (*Rep.* X.611d). Shame reaches deep down in the morally learned soul and implants the compelling question that raises ontological doubt: *what kind of creature am I* that I have *done* this thing? Just at our weakest moments, when we need all our moral tools, and all the guidance and support we can glean from our moral teachers, shame shows up to dehumanize us.

Shame is a moral teacher that teaches only those who do not need its lessons. Its moral lessons are lost on those worst of characters, those who most need its teaching. But shame has greater flaws than its mere ineffectiveness on tyrants and fools. The greatest danger is that those members of the moral choir to whom shame is actively preaching can easily over-learn their lessons. Shame's ontological demotion scolds the conscientious: "Bad me!" "Inadequate me!" "Morally corrupt me!" These messages gnaw away at the morally learned heart, destroying the morally sensitive soul, and disfiguring her moral fiber. The good can take shame's warning too deeply to heart, and can retire, as did Achilles, from the moral battlefield, or throw themselves on the side of the enemy, as did the disgraced Alkibiades when he discovered his inappropriate love for Socrates to be shameful.

Shame is a useful moral tool if it warns us, as Socrates' *daimonion* does, in advance of a moral lapse. It can act as our guide, boost our moral confidence, and help us to be more effective decision-makers and exemplars to the morally struggling. But where the error is made and cannot be undone, shame is unhelpful in helping us to move forward from the failures that are an inevitable aspect of the human condition. It is just one, but I believe the most destructive, of the many debilitating affects—resentment, hatred, blame, envy, greed—that undermine a person's fundamental joy in existence, her sense of worth, and her capacity to relate to others compassionately.

CHAPTER TWELVE. PHILOSOPHICAL TREATMENTS FOR THE SICKLY DAEMON

We have seen that destructive affects such as shame do not make healthy pedagogical tools to school people in right conduct. Shame simply does not work very well on those who most need its moral lessons. But this incapacity is not its greatest failing. Far more dangerous is the capacity of shame to work *too well* on those whose hearts are open, vulnerable to criticism, and prone to self-denigration and despair about their moral development. To those who most deeply desire to avert ethical mistakes, as they walk the morally treacherous paths of their imperfect human lives, shame touches a sore spot very deep in the psyche that may never completely heal.

In *The Art of Happiness*, Western psychiatrist Howard C. Cutler discusses with the Dalai Lama the tendency for Western practitioners to fall into a paralyzing despair when they recognize their moral failure. Cutler asks the sage if he has ever experienced feelings of guilt about errors he has made along the way of his life, when he recognizes that he has made mistakes that he cannot go back and change. The Dalai Lama assures Cutler that his life has not been exempt from error. He tells the story of a mistake he made when counseling an older monk, a hermit and an accomplished Buddhist. The Dalai Lama tells Cutler that the old monk came to him to receive advanced teachings, but he advised him in such a way that it cost the old monk his life. His Holiness tells:

> [The old monk] came to me one day and asked me about doing a certain high-level esoteric practice. I remarked in a casual way that this would be a difficult practice and would perhaps be better undertaken by someone who was younger, that traditionally it was a practice that should be started in one's midteens.[1]

His Holiness recalls that he didn't think any more about it until the news reached him, after a while, that "the monk had killed himself in order to be reborn in a younger body to more effectively undertake the practice."[2]

The psychiatrist was shocked on hearing his Holiness' story. "However did you get rid of that feeling?" Cutler wonders, and presses the holy man for his secrets in battling the shame of failure. "I didn't get rid of it. It's still there," the Dalai Lama answered. The sage recognizes what we ordinary people miss: that guilt for moral error must not be permitted to get in the way of future moral success. Interpreting the holy man's insight into the language of his disciplinary field, Cutler offers his analysis:

> Guilt arises when we convince ourselves that we have made an irreparable mistake. The torture of guilt is in thinking that any problem is permanent. Since there is nothing that does not change, so too pain subsides— a problem doesn't persist.[3]

Cutler's profession surely offers him ample opportunity to witness the destructive effects of guilt and shame on human lives. Thus, the Buddhist insight of impermanence is granted very practical application in Cutler's counsel that we not burden ourselves with false ideas about the permanence of our effects. Even our worst mistakes are just passing things. Though we cannot go back and change what we have done or erase the effects we have had on others, our mistakes are simply fleeting

---

1 Dalai Lama and Howard C. Cutler, *The Art of Happiness: A Handbook for Living* (New York: Riverhead Books, 1998), p. 161.
2 Ibid.
3 Ibid., pp. 162-63.

realities, brief moments in time. So the best advice is to regret our mistakes and then, like the Dalai Lama, leave them in the past where they belong.

The Dalai Lama is one of many Tibetan Buddhist teachers who have been laboring to import Buddhist ideas to the Western world. These teachers began to notice something peculiar to Western practitioners that is foreign in Easterners. His student, American Buddhist nun Pema Chödron, Acharya of Gampo Abbey in Nova Scotia and student of Chogyam Trungpa Rinpoche, a primary teacher charged with bringing Buddhism to the West, tells that the Tibetans "were not prepared for the likes of us!" How are we Westerners different? The Buddhist dharma and especially the Noble Eightfold path are designed to guide practitioners' life paths so they may realize fundamental happiness, by breaking free of the crippling addictions of a grasping and craving life through the cultivation of compassion and wisdom about the true nature of things as fleeting and changeable. Guidelines for the spiritual journey, called "precepts," are meant to open up the practitioner's vision of the world beyond the narrow categories of good and bad, right and wrong, friend and foe, ego and other. Meditation upon the self and the nature of reality leads to recognition of the common moral frailty that links all human beings, so meditative practices are designed to free people from the judgmentalism that divides the world and show them that all beings are fluid and fluctuating realities, determined by causes and conditions.

Eastern practitioners tend to accept the precepts as helpful guidelines for enhancing positive qualities ("virtues") and diminishing negative qualities ("vices"), trusting in their fundamental goodness ("Buddhanature") to support them along their path to happiness ("enlightenment"). But Westerners, the Tibetan teachers soon noticed, have a strong propensity to turn the precepts against themselves. They take the gentle guidelines of the precepts and apply them as a rigorous asceticism. Then, when they fail, as people inevitably will along a lifelong path, we Westerners denigrate ourselves as "vice-ridden," sink into shame and self-loathing, declare ourselves failures, unworthy of happiness and step off the path altogether. Or we get it right and adopt the precepts successfully, then straightway declare our-

selves "virtuous," become proud and arrogant about our progress, and appalled and disgusted by the others who are doing it
wrong.

Tibetans, from the Dalai Lama to Trungpa and Chödron, have
taken upon themselves the delicate task of redesigning Buddhist practice "for the likes of us." They find they cannot use the
usual teaching terms (virtues and vices, austerities, confession,
refraining) without painstakingly undercutting their meanings.
Otherwise, we Westerners shame ourselves into virtue and
shame others for their vices. Chödron undercuts the rigor of the
precepts by telling us stories about how *not* to be rigid and in-
transigent as we tread the spiritual path. I paraphrase from her
"Happiness" lecture:

> A man is beating his dog and practically killing it.
> One day the dog shows up at your door. And you take
> the dog and you hide it. When the dog's owner comes to
> your door, you tell him you haven't seen the dog. So you
> actually lie and you keep the dog and don't give it back
> to the owner. You have not been honest with a neighbor
> and you have taken what has not been given. Do you
> get all fretful because you have lied and you have sto-
> len? Not at all. You know perfectly well that you have
> helped to avert harm doing.

Chödron closes her story in her familiar breezy way: *And
that's kind of the way it is.*

The Tibetans find that the biggest obstacle to Westerners'
developing a compassionate orientation toward others and plot-
ting a common path to world peace resides in widespread underlying insecurities and a weak sense of self-worth. We share
a common tendency toward self-denigration and we are highly
prone toward discrediting ourselves and others. We share a
common sense of shame, deep down in our souls, that easily triggers negative responses which can turn aggressive and violent.

It is significant that the Tibetan teachers have found in
Westerners precisely what psychologists have discovered to
be the single most common feature connecting perpetrators of
violent crime. Studies show unequivocally that domestic and
intimate violence offenders, as well as perpetrators of other vio-

lent crimes, have generally been abused in childhood or made to witness the abuse of loved ones (generally a mother or sibling). As a result, they are left with a stinging sense of shame for their inability to protect themselves and others from harm, a sense of their moral failing in situations of dire need. Their burden of shame configures them for hypervigilance and mistrust of themselves and others, and rage at a world so menacing. They carry their shame out into the world where it rebounds as violence upon innocent others.[1]

Shame is a weapon that has been wielded throughout the history of the West to bring people down off their high horses and keep them in moral line. Parents have used it, teachers have used it, priests have used it, warmongering presidents have used it to press citizens onto the battlefield. Shame after the losses of World War One drove Germany into the excesses of National Socialism and into the Holocaust. The Protestant ethic, which still frames the American worldview today, uses shame to blame people for their poverty and motivate the "lazy" and "indigent" poor to work diligently within a system that fails them. But shame's paradoxical pedagogical force propels people, who have nothing morally to lose, toward crime as a means of overcoming their shameful impoverishment in a prosperous society, and toward a violent catharsis of their rage.

Shame is a useful weapon of moral teaching when it is self-applied to warn us against our impending moral errors. But it is altogether unhelpful in putting right our past failures and helping us to move forward from them. Shame *may* be useful, but it can never *be used* to good ends. When shame is applied externally, when we shame others for not doing what *we* think they should, we create the conditions that give rise to self-loathing, rage, crime, violence, and war.

Buddhism counsels, in place of the debilitating negative affects (*kleshas*) that cause us to despair, and ultimately to strike out to harm ourselves and others, an attitude of loving-kindness (*maitri* in Pali, *metta* in Sanskrit). *Maitri* is the basis for developing the "good heart" that is the soil for cultivating compassion for responding to suffering others. But *maitri* begins with the

1 See especially Linda G. Mills, *Violent Partners*, pp. 93-97.

self. We must love ourselves before we can love the others, just as empty hands cannot feed the hungry. Thus, the new forms of Buddhism for guilt-ridden, virtue-mourning, shameful Westerners urges self-love and gentleness along the path of mindful awareness. Because we, as all beings, are fundamentally good, radiant drops in the vast ocean of Being that Buddhists call "Buddhanature," we all have ample reason to feel perfect, despite all the mistakes we make along the way of our lives. As Suzuki Roshi, the founder of the San Francisco Zen Center, said to a sea of faces who had come to hear him speak: *You are all perfect just as you are—and you could use a little work.*

We could all use a little moral work. But the mourning hedgehog and the shamefaced hostage continue to enlist the unhealthy affects that are varied aspects of shame (*aiskhuron*) that the Greeks oppose to *kalos* (beauty). To be ashamed is to feel ugly, repulsive to others. In the Western tradition, we tend to feel ugly and repulsive for our failures. Levinas and Derrida seek to depart from an unhelpful ethical tradition extending from the Greeks, but ironically their ethics of guilt, shame, and mourning keeps them steadfastly in the Greek ethical camp.[1] Shaming failure is a throw-back to a barbaric age, when warriors ruled the polis and inquisitors the temple. When loving-kindness to self and others frames the moral path, our failures become the fruitful ground of spiritual and moral practice, enhancing our self-awareness, humbling our arrogance, and augmenting our understanding of other people's weaknesses, as we all struggle against common challenges to scale the steep ascent to human justice. Self-love props up the self against hopelessness and promotes the compassion for others that undergirds world peace.

We have seen that Julia Kristeva holds out little hope for love as an enduring force that survives the test of time. She describes but two possible futures for the lovers, neither of which satisfies our intuitive sense of what love is. Either time turns love's passion cold, leaving the couple to a tired and cynical collusion, or else the lovers maintain the passion of their connection through recurrent cycles of masochism and sadism. The message underlying both alternatives is that love has not the power to endure

---

1 *Aiskuros* (shame) the Greeks link to *aiskroteis*, the deformed, and oppose to the beautiful, *kalos*.

the endless routine of the everyday. No matter how tightly the lovers hold onto each other, time changes their circumstances. Time changes their love, snuffing it out or sickening it into pathology.

Time is threatening to lovers because it brings change and fear of change can drive them to distorted worldviews and obsessive behaviors. Intimate abuse is often motivated by the commendable, but unrealistic, goal of preserving love against the ravages of time. Intimates behaving badly, according to this explanation, are simply struggling to hold back the tide of time by controlling changing circumstances, waning passions, and shifting relationships. Many of the symptoms of sickening love suggest that this battle against time and change may be the motivator of oppression.

One of the earliest, and most frequent, symptoms of abuse in intimate relations is the increasing isolation of the weaker party from her larger social context. The abusive partner will progressively discourage or forbid his partner contact with friends and family, until he ultimately gains absolute control over her movements, her allegiances, and her behaviors. But the primary goal is not mere bodily compliance to his commands; he seeks control over her view of their shared reality. He seeks control of her interpretation of her situation. The abuser can break her bones and bruise her flesh, but as long as a victim is capable of recognizing that these acts are unjust, the violent partner has not won the fullest conquest over his victim. The deepest harm is the one that seeps into the victim's psyche and convinces her that she deserves this treatment, that her tyrant is acting out of love for her, that he is her protector and not her tyrant.

Emmanuel Levinas writes of this tragic situation in the essay "Freedom and Command."[1] In this essay, Levinas begins from Plato, who configures freedom as the freedom of reason to rise above external circumstances. In this configuration, tyranny can only be understood as control over the body of another. People can be tyrannized precisely because their matter, their animality, leaves them vulnerable to others, open to suffering. Socrates escapes the vulnerability of flesh in drinking the hemlock, be-

---

1 Emmanuel Levinas, *Collected Philosophical Papers* (Dordecht, Netherlands: Kluwer Academic, 1986), pp. 15-23.

cause as "his body becomes progressively benumbed," his reason is released from the body's servitude, from its entanglement
with external circumstances, from its vulnerability to suffering.
Reason soars freely, as the body's sensibilities wane and cease
their interference with its workings.[1]

In this essay, Levinas seeks to show that Plato's understanding of tyranny is stunted. To understand the full reach of tyranny, we must consider the way that external powers weigh down
upon our freedom. Tyrants have their effects not only upon our
bodies, but in the worst cases, their will seeps into our psyches
and alters our very reason. Tyranny's domain, argues Levinas, is
extensive of all that we are and everything that we own. The
breadth of tyranny's reach is explained by the number of "tools"
at tyranny's disposal: "the possibilities of tyranny are much more
extensive [than Plato allows]. . . . It has unlimited resources at
its disposal, those of love and wealth, torture and hunger, silence
and rhetoric."[2]

In Plato's account in the *Phaedo*, it is the body which comes
into view as vulnerable. Again in the *Statesman*, Plato has the
young fool Polus boast that orators are as powerful as tyrants,
because both are capable of "putting to death anyone they
please, and depriving anyone of his property, and expelling him
from their cities as they see fit."[3] The worst consequences that
Plato can imagine, it seems, have to do with loss of life, loss of
property, and exile. But Levinas recognizes that tyranny's grasp
extends well beyond the flesh and material possessions. Of the
tools he places at tyranny's disposal, only torture, hunger, and
(to some degree) wealth have claim upon the body. Love, silence,
and rhetoric—their effects eat away at the very soul, cripple the
reason that Plato envisions escaping death and bringing freedom.

The tools of tyranny that enslave the psyche are far subtler
and craftier instruments than racks and thumbscrews. Gently,
oh so gently, love and its handmaidens, silence and rhetoric, act
to manage truth; they colonize the victim's psyche, until her reason is no longer her own, no longer essentially free, but given
over to the beloved. "The supreme violence is the supreme gen-

---

1 Ibid., p. 16.
2 Ibid. p. 16.
3 Plato, *Statesman* 466c.

tleness," states Levinas. "To have a servile soul is to be incapable of being jarred, incapable of being ordered."[1]

The soul is incapable of being jarred or ordered, not because of its essential nature as freedom, not because its autonomy is insuperable, but by virtue of a logical paradox: love causes all wishes to be granted in advance, so nothing remains to be taken. Love is the greatest tool of tyranny because in the extreme of its hold, the lover willingly sacrifices her life, her freedom, her property, her birth name and hence her family, her city, her country, and all other allegiances. Nothing remains to be seized. Levinas describes this colonizing, suffocating love in spatial terms: "The love for the master fills the soul to such an extent that the soul no longer takes its distance."[2]

"Servile souls" fail to keep appropriate distance; they do not observe reasonable boundaries, they pull up the stakes and cast down the fences that make for reasonable relations. The lover loves too intensely, too closely, places every resource at the service of the beloved. In so doing, she erases the relationship of tyranny, by aligning her will with the will of her tyrant. The supreme tyranny, after all, is no tyranny at all. "Violent action does not consist in being in a relationship with another; it is in fact an action where one is as though one were alone."[3]

Love can only occur where there are two—lover and beloved. Where the will of the beloved, however subtle, creeps in and inhabits the will of the beloved, colonizing her reason and annulling her difference, love and tyranny are no longer. "Darling, I wish you would stay in with me tonight!" but the tyrant is alone with himself. Only *his* will is present, only his *conatus* active. Plato confirms this paradox in the *Republic*'s analysis of the tyrant, when he declares the tyrant the loneliest of men.

Love cannot exist where there is only one. But it also cannot survive too much multiplicity. Empedocles of Acragas, a Pre-Socratic philosopher, offers a cosmological vision that can help us in our understanding of the one/many problem of love that collapses into the solipsism of tyranny. Empedocles' poem, *On Nature*, is responding to Parmenides' earlier poem *The Way of*

1 E. Levinas, *Collected Philosophical Papers*, p. 16.
2 Ibid.
3 Ibid., p. 19.

Truth, which describes the philosopher's dream journey to the heavens where the goddess Justice apprises him of the truth of things, a truth missed by mere mortals. The truth is contained in dual propositions about Being, so powerful that they raise a roadblock to future philosophy: "that *it is* and cannot *not be.*"[1] The upshot of this divine message is that Being is a single, whole, undivided reality, uncreated and everlasting. "One way only is left to be spoken of, that *it is.* . . uncreated and imperishable, and without end . . . it is now, all at once, one continuous."[2]

Empedocles sets out to meet Parmenides' dual challenge that "reality cannot come from unreality nor plurality from an original unity" by denying the original unity.[3] Empedocles posits four eternal but distinct substances, Zeus, Hera, Aidoneus, and Nestis (Fire, Air, Earth, and Water). All the world of things consist of these "four roots" mixed in varying proportions—a universe of differences built upon common indestructible elements, temporarily drawn together and then dissolved. Change and motion in space are mere rearrangements of the fundamental elements. But what motivates their rearrangement? Empedocles accounts for the reshuffling of the four base elements by introducing two primary motive forces, Love and Strife (Philotēti and Neikeos).

> A double tale I will tell: at one time it grew to be one only from many, at another it divided again to be many from one. There is a double coming into being of mortal things and a double passing away. One is brought about, and again destroyed, by the coming together of all things, the other grows up and is scattered as things are again divided. And these things never cease from continual shifting, at one time all coming together, through Love, at another each borne apart from the others through Strife.[4]

1 Fr. 2, Proclus *in Tim.* I, 345, 18 Diehl. Cited in G. S. Kirk and J. E. Raven, *The Presocratic Philosophers* (London: Cambridge University Press, 1957), p. 269.
2 Fr. 8, Simplicius *Phys.* 145, I. Cited in Kirk and Raven *The Presocratic Philosophers,* p. 273.
3 Kirk and Raven, *The Presocratic Philosophers,* p. 324.
4 Fr. 17, 1-13, Simplicius *Phys.* 158, 1. Cited in Kirk and Raven *The Presocratic Philosophers,* p. 326.

Empedocles' poem maintains the wholeness of the world, in compliance with Parmenides' dictum, but his founding plurality allows for the changes across time that explain mortal existence. The poem is a cosmological tale, but it has explanatory power over all beginnings and endings. The cycles Empedocles foretells for things, in contrast to Kristeva's dark prediction, sees love as a foundational power of the universe, drawing together elements to bring beings into being, and drawing together those beings into larger unities—families, communities and neighborhoods, nations, and at the highest level of unity, the fullness of created life, the world as we know it at any given moment. In the early eons of Love's reign, all things are gathered together, in such a dynamic, vital way that its individual parts are preserved *as individual* even as the whole comes together as one, on many different levels. When Love first rules the universe, all things are as one, but preserve their individual plurality. Love, according to Empedocles' reckoning, is the creative force of the universe, "the cause of good things."[1] It causes things to come into being; it holds them together in integrity. Love is also "inborn in mortal limbs."[2] We think kind thoughts, perform deeds of accord, and bring joy to our fellows through Love's beneficial influence.[3]

But ultimately Love goes too far. It pulls separate things together, closer and closer, until everything melts into one and differences are obliterated. A congealed mass, a faceless bulk, an orb of fiery mud, in Love's fullness, Parmenidean Being returns with a vengeance—still, lifeless being. At this point in the cosmology, the opposite force, Strife, must enter and separate out each element again. For a while, life and world arise again from Love's suffocating embrace. But as Strife's reign goes on, a contrary tragedy follows: separately existent things are slowly pulled to pieces. Communities are split, families are torn, and ultimately individual creatures tear each other limb from limb.

What is Empedocles' message for our lovers? Love functions best where it draws individuals together in joyful accord,

---

1 Aristotle *Met.* A4, 985 a4. (DK 31 A 39). Cited in Kirk and Raven *The Presocratic Philosophers*, p. 330.
2 Fr. 17, l. 14, Simplicius *Phys.* 158, 13. Cited in Kirk and Raven *The Presocratic Philosophers*, p. 328.
3 Aristotle *Met.* □9, 1075 b1. Cited in Kirk and Raven *The Presocratic Philosophers*, p. 330.

where strong communities support their members in reaching their fullest potential. But too much love is dangerous. Great care must be taken to preserve a healthy distance between one thing and another, because love has a tendency to exceed the bounds of the reasonable and snuff out individuality and even life. Too much love, too much clinging and congealing, too much smothering and stifling, and distinctions begin to blur. It grows unclear where one thing breaks off and the next thing starts. The air grows thick, the waters muddy, and intimacy begins to feel like death. Panic sets in and drives us to crave strife as the only exit from Being.

A domicile is just a house until love enters to christen it a home. A home needs enough closeness between individual members to guarantee an adequate degree of sameness to establish a sense of common identity. Common markers of identity ensure continued interactions that bring the familiar joy of "like" company. Love is the ontological glue that renders a house a home. On the other hand, love is an adhesive that requires air to make its bond. If the glue is too thick, if the bond too tight, the gap between the lovers closes and the homespace withers and sickens. Love becomes a daemon in the sanctuary. The daemon, in Plato's myth, son of Poverty and Plenty; it is a monster half-god caught between the extremes of too much and too little. The result is homespace violence, the most agonizing, the most lethal, the most tragic of violences, and the hardest one to cure. Once the reign of Strife sets in, it knows no limits. It tears worlds to bloody shreds. Where people have drawn the closest—in the intimate family setting—the danger is greatest.

CHAPTER FOURTEEN. THE PSYCHOTHERAPIST'S DAEMON

Before we have loved and lost, we are as babies fresh from the womb. Nurtured and protected, we feel ourselves the center-point of the universe. Warnings to take care with our hearts have an unreal quality, like a fairytale. We trust in our vast network of support systems—loved ones, custom, the law, the structure of the civilized world—to protect us and guarantee that only good things happen to good people. Psychologists offer a compelling history to this in fallible sense of self. They trace the organizing structure of our fundamental relationships with the world to our infancy, when we saw the world through a narcissistic haze of satisfaction and utter self-interest. It is not simply that everyone *other* exists for *my* welfare; it is rather that in our earliest understanding, no *other* exists at all. For the newborn infant, there is the sure sense that we are all there is, self-sufficient in our ability to call forth a dry diaper when we feel wet, food when we are hungry, and warm blankets or cuddles when we are cold.

Primary narcissism, which has as its original source the unencumbered union of infant and mother, orients our being-in-the-world. It gives us a sense of ourselves as the center point of being that endures long after we learn the truth—that mother is a separate being who does not always jump to my needs at my command. Nonetheless, the original perfect narcissism stays with us as a model on which we measure ourselves, our lives, and our loves. Epstein confirms:

The original feeling of unity persists in the psyche as a driving force toward which the person aspires in adult life. Both in love relations and in our subjective sense of ourselves we attempt to re-create or recapture that original feeling of infantile perfection from which we have all been inexorably divorced.[1]

Our earliest human encounter leaves us haunted by the lost perfection of the original mother-infant unity, where ego was the governing center of all that existed, whose command brought the fulfillment of all needs and desires—milk, dry clothing, loving touch, and positive emotional feedback. The original union is the foundation of the "pleasure principle" according to which all future experience will be measured. Psychologists track the fate of this union in the developing life of the ego: with consciousness of self as distinct from other, the perfect primary union bifurcates into a confused and unhappy split—on the one hand is the "object libido," in which the ego understands other people as the source of its happiness, and on the other hand is the "ego libido," where the ego's hopes and dreams for fulfillment and happiness are rooted only in the self. A sense of loss haunts the developing ego and its work becomes the critical task of healing the unhappy split and regaining the lost wholeness of primary infancy. Epstein tells, "In the attempt to preserve this illusion of security, the ego races back and forth between the two extremes of fullness and emptiness, hoping that one or the other will provide the necessary refuge."[2]

The ego's development toward a state of happiness, a sense of wellbeing and feelings of authentic completion, rests on the shaky ground that joins these two conflicted forces or energies ("object libido" and "ego libido"). The conflict can only be resolved by what psychologists name "sublimation," which is really not anything "sub" at all, but a movement *upward*—a synthesis of the Hegelian type. The ego must raise itself above the fray of the two conflicting drives and transform their clashing energies

---

1 Mark Epstein, *Thoughts Without a Thinker* (New York: MJF Books, 1995), p. 81.
2 Ibid., p. 70.

into "a higher state or plane of existence."[1] Epstein traces the rising path that seeks to unify and heal the inner rift:

> We are all haunted by the lost perfection of the ego that contained everything, and we measure ourselves and our lovers against this standard. We search for a replica in external satisfactions, in food, comfort, sex, or success, but gradually learn, through the process of sublimation, that the best approximation for that lost feeling comes from creative acts that evoke states of being in which self-consciousness is temporarily relinquished.[2]

So we can find moments of satisfaction beyond the conflicted drives only by self-forgetting, by releasing our desperate grasp upon those tormenting needs. Focusing on others can help with that release. But it is crucial to understand that the force that drives us toward human connection is not the blindly self-forgetting adoration for a singular beloved, but the drive for our own completion and release from our internally split selves. We think that our adorations are about the other and his needs, but ultimately the truth of love is a self-serving truth, one captured in the famous love line that Jerry Maguire (played by Tom Cruise) expresses in the love story bearing the lead character's name: *You complete me.* The "me" does not disappear in homage to the "you" so much as the "you" is swallowed up in accomplishing the completed "me."

Epstein explains that psychology recognizes two fundamental currents of life energy driving human beings forward—the subjective yearning self, or "ego libido," which sees itself as the self-sufficient receptacle of all its hopes and dreams; and the objective self, the "object libido," which looks to others to complete itself and fulfill its dreams of perfection.[3] This psychological account of life's dual currents of energy suggests that a person is caught between two morally hard places: blind self-assertion

---

1 Hans Loewald, *Sublimation: Inquiries into Theoretical Psychoanalysis* (New Haven, Conn.: Yale University Press, 1988), p. 13. Cited by Epstein, *Thoughts Without a Thinker*, p. 82.
2 Epstein, *Thoughts Without a Thinker*, p. 82.
3 Ibid., p. 82.

and aggressive consumption of others. Epstein navigates these two rocky poles to locate an antidote for these destructive energies in the Buddhist practice of naked, honest, nonjudgmental self-awareness—meditation—which cultivates alternative, higher order values for skillful living: wisdom and compassion.

> Wisdom is, after all, sublimated ego libido; it is investment in the self turned inside out, the transformation of narcissism and the eradication of ignorance about the nature of self. What kind of conceit is possible after all, when the self . . . is understood as already broken? Compassion, it follows, is sublimated object libido: desire and rage transformed through the vision of there being no separate subject in need of a magical reunion with either a gratifying or a frustrating Other.[1]

In the next chapter we shall consider the harm effected by the sickly daemon as consistent with any trauma, leaving the agonized victim in the state that psychotherapists label Post-Traumatic Stress Disorder (PTSD).

---

1 Ibid.

CHAPTER FIFTEEN. HEALING THE SICKLY DAEMON

Our study of romantic idealizations of love has revealed the deep philosophical roots, thousands of years old, that underpin the unrealistically lofty expectations about love that people continue to cling today. Ancient philosophers, such as Plato, have presented love as all-suffering and all-enduring, and moreover worthy of any amount of misery and torment. The philosophical myths suggest that this daemon might well land us in the streets, wandering barefoot and sleeping in doorways, but even at this high cost, love is worth every wretchedness, every pain, and every loss, if these troubles and woundings and struggles serve to keep our passion alive.

We have seen that Hollywood has grasped onto these mythologems and communicated them to a broad public audience—and mostly to a young female audience. As a result of romantic films and romance novels, young people—and especially young women—grow up blinded by the seductive mythologies a result, they are poorly prepared for what love actually is. They learn very early on that love is a divine madness, a festival that sets them apart from, and above, the routine chores and duties of the everyday. When the everyday sets in, they are devastated by the idea that the love has died and short of divorce, they do not know where to turn to reignite the flame.

In the feminist philosophies that have arisen over recent decades, the holes in the fabric of love's mythology have begun to be revealed. We have come to see a darker side of love, its lofty promises tied up with tyranny and abuse. Kristeva's study of love's possible futures, in *Tales of Love*, left room for no happy endings for the lovers. For Kristeva, everyday life is the absolute challenge for love, from which Romeo and Juliet's remedy— death—proves the easy way out. If the lovers choose life, there remain only two ways of going forward, across the grinding hours and days of mundane marital existence: the lovers become locked into "a tired and cynical collusion" or their love will sicken into cycles of sadomasochism that wound them and others around them. This is not a choice between boredom and passion, but a choice between two forms of torment. The humdrum, passionless everydayness represents a protracted, excruciating torture, where the lovers trudge on day after day, steeped in resentment and regret, while the second alternative sees a "monstrous couple," who keep their passion alive by indulging in endless cycles of cruelty, occasionally pulling third-party victims into their love's fetid sequences.

Kristeva's study of the lovers' dual fate reveals the danger zones of love that might explain why violence has an overwhelming tendency to erupt in the homespace. She has frustrated our hopes, not only for realizing love's loftier ideals, but for achieving any relationship that meets our intuitive sense of what love is. Sadomasochism and cynicism simply do not fulfill even our most minimal expectations of the daemon. Kristeva has left no room for a strong and robust love that stands the test of time and provides opportunity for the festival of passionate escape, but in such a way that the everyday routines of family life are confirmed and renewed. This healthier love is what is required if both love's passion and the daily order of family life are to endure the alchemy of time.

To secure a happier ending for our lovers in a story of wholesome intimate relations, we must first abandon our unrealistic ideals about what love ought to be. It is especially crucial that we abandon those mythologems, which configure suffering as due and rightful payment for love. Having abandoned suffering as a fitting rubric for explaining enduring love, let us chart a path for our lovers that winds between the two courses Kristeva cites. We must rescue our lovers from the passionless cynicism of love's promises lost, without landing them in the dangerous cyclical enthusiasm of sadomasochistic love. To chart this careful course for our lovers, it will be helpful to turn to experts in the field of couples therapy to identify the strategies which they recommend to lovers who have become caught up in cycles of sadomasochism, to teach them how to maintain the passion that we intuitively associate with love without sacrificing their physical, emotional, and mental welfare.

Before we begin our exploration of sadomasochism's cure, a few disclaimers are needed. First, although judges in the United States refer thousands of convicted intimate abusers to violence intervention programs every year, these programs are for the most part unsuccessful. They do not rupture the cycles of intimate violence that they are designed to break. The programs do not work, but if they did, they still would reach only the tiny tip of an enormous iceberg of domestic violence that is widespread across the United States. The violent partners who end up in U.S. courts are but a fraction of the actual mass of offenders; as many as 75% of battered women do not call in the authorities when their partners are violent. If we are to chart a path that leads between the two unhappy paths that Kristeva predicts for our lovers, we must understand more fully what goes wrong in the current programs for treating intimate violence.

We have seen that Linda G. Mills takes up the question of curing sickened intimate relations in her *Violent Partners*. In this work, she tracks rigorous studies of batterer intervention programs and explains their general failure as a failure of the general philosophy of intimate violence as conceived by the "battered women's movement" and a consequent misguided methodology for treatment research that has become encoded in judicial policy. Mills argues for a new methodology for treating intimate violence. Intimate violence research shows unequivocally that current approaches do not work. It is true that those offenders who find themselves faced with huge existential and financial losses as a result of their abusive behaviors, such as losing jobs, homes, families, and reputations, do prove less likely to reoffend after completing intervention programs. But studies show too the highly troubling fact that offenders have the tendency to drop out of the programs long before completion, and when they do drop out, they are more likely to reoffend than those who do not receive treatment at all.[1]

Mills' fundamental criticism of current intervention programs for domestic abuse is that they target only the abusive (that is, generally male) partner, remove him from the family setting, and then seek to change his behavior by appealing to his self-interest, the losses that accompany violent behavior. This approach fails because at no point does the program seek to alter the offenders' fundamental beliefs about the appropriateness of violence as a response to daily frustrations with their partners. "[M]en didn't change their attitudes about violence after attending the entire program—even when they became less violent."[2] Studies show that abusive males change their behaviors only if they stand to suffer significant losses, but the concerns of self-interest do not affect the underlying assumptions and worldview that motivate the behaviors in the first place.

> [T]here was no noted change in attitudes toward domestic violence after completing either program [eight week short programs or twenty-six week longer programs]. In other words, the reform was based on behavior modification as a result of perceived or possible negative outcomes ("I better do this or I'm going to be in more trouble") rather than on a new understanding that hurting one's partner is wrong ("I now see my violence and my relationship in an entirely different light and accept responsibility for my actions").[3]

Mills takes a radically unorthodox approach to curing intimate violence, and her approach has been met with vigorous criticism from the community of psychological experts treating domestic abuse. The reason for Mills' cold reception is that her method challenges the founding worldview of the "battered women's movement" which states that aggressive men beat innocent women. Framing domestic violence as a dynamic pattern

1 Mills, *Violent Partners*. p. 37. c.f. p. 205.
2 Ibid., p. 37.
3 Ibid.

of interaction between two partners or within a community of actors, Mills as well contravenes one of the cardinal laws of abuse response: never ask about the victim. To explain, cure, or contain intimate violence, the traditional approach insists, police, courts, and therapists must look only at the perpetrator. In the dominant worldview of domestic violence experts, to ask about the victim, her identity or behaviors, is tantamount to "blaming the victim." Asking about the victim suggests raising doubt as to the victim's status as "innocent" and undeserving of her fate. Because of the expert community's flat refusal to implicate the victim as a causal force in the violence, judges not only avoid ordering couples therapy as a solution to domestic violence; in some states such an order is illegal.

Mills explains that the battered women's movement from the beginning framed their lobbying against domestic abuse around the goal of empowering women victims. Since intimate violence was, in their view, defined as "aggressive misogynistic males attacking innocent women," the only appropriate response to intimate violence was to break the abusive marriage apart, once and for all. The feminists' goal was explicit: to empower women to reject altogether the abusive relationship, dump the man and begin life anew. The problem arises when we realize that many women do not want to leave their abusive lovers. A response system designed to break up abusive relationships fails to reach the woman who does not share this predetermined goal. Moreover, the founding assumptions of the system occlude a growing victim group, the battered male partner, whose numbers now exceed 800,000 per year in the United States.

Many women who seek protection from an abusive partner do not share the system goals for them. They do not seek release from the abusive partnership; they simply want the violence to end. A multitude of reasons keep them committed to the relationship: family integrity highly valued above personal safety, fear of losing their children or their home, low self-esteem, financial fears, deep investment in the relationship, love and pity for the sick partner.

Some victims are simply too weak, after long periods of abuse, to break free from the clutches of a passionate bond, even where the passion is sickened. But more often than not, the victims of abuse are not simply physical victims of their abusive partner but mental victims as well. The weaker partner will often share the worldview of the stronger, believing herself to deserve the abuse. "If only I were not such a terrible wife, if only I did not burn the dinner, if only I raised the children the way my husband wants, I would not be causing all this family upset." In instances of abuse where the victim's worldview has been successfully colonized with the logic of abuse, the feminist demand for the woman's clean break from her abusers simply adds to the list of her failures the shame of her inability to permanently fix the situation.

In still other cases, the victims know something is terribly wrong, they recognize that the danger will likely escalate, and that their children are being harmed by exposure to the violence. But they still do not want out. They seek to cure—not to kill—their sickened relationships. They may indeed have a keen awareness of their active role in the escalating violence, while not sharing the sickened worldview of the abuser that blames her for everything that happens.

There are many diverse scenarios to explain why the vast majority of intimate violence victims fail to report their abuse, and why, of those who do report and are removed to the safety of shelters, more than half of the women will return to their violent homes. A system that will force them toward ends they do not seek is not a system that serves them. Mills attempts to close the gap in the system, by providing services to suit the situations of the great numbers of women (and men) who choose to remain in their dangerous situations and work to overcome the violence.

Mills' understanding of intimate violence recalls Kristeva's description of sadomasochistic love, where cycles of violence preserve the passion in the lovers' sickened love life. Mills looks at intimate violence as a dynamic process that unfolds according to certain patterns of beliefs and behaviors, taken up by both parties. If the couple wants to stay together, after all that they have been through, then refusing them couples counseling closes the door of support altogether. Declining to ask questions about the victim makes it difficult to understand not only the evolution of the cycles of violence that are played out between the partners, but also the psychological history that motivates a victim to stay in, and perhaps even seek out, abusive partnerships. Victimhood, like perpetration, can stalk people throughout their lives. If the cycles of abuse are to be stopped once and for all, the therapist must understand how broad and deep the behavioral cycles run and what each member of the conflict contributes toward the escalating cycles of violence.

Mills' innovative approach lets new issues come to light that are hidden in traditional frameworks for understanding the problem of intimate violence. Much stands to be gained by broadening the scope of research to include the behavior of women in cycles of intimate violence. Mills underscores "the value for women of recognizing their contribution to the violence in their lives; the fluidity often found between the roles of victim and victimizer; the significance of seeing violent men as potentially capable of change."[1]

The fact that more and more male victims are coming forward to reveal the details of their situations suggests that at least in some cases, women are not simply the passive sufferers of male aggression, but turn to specific forms of violence that better suit their (sometimes inferior) physical abilities. If they can overcome the taboo about questioning the female role in family violence, researchers will no doubt enjoy growing opportunities to study the specific forms of female violence and study their frequency.

Mills' method for interrupting the cycles of violence in intimate relations is instructive for our understanding of how to arrive at a healthy love which might support, rather than undermine and sacrifice, familial peace. Mills believes in "holistic, meaningful treatment options that give couples the choice of confronting their violence together."[2] She seeks an approach that is as broad as possible, including the whole family to address cycles of abuse that may stretch across generations. Under the rubric of "restorative justice," Mills brings the paradigm of social sickness and healing to bear on the couples' violence.

Restorative justice imagines bringing everyone in a room together to discuss the effects of a particular

1 Ibid., pp. 204-05.
2 Ibid. 205.

crime on their lives. It has given rise to many different sorts of specific programs around the world designed to promote healing among the affected parties after acts of violence. Its goal is to help the group develop insights together on what happened among them and why so that everyone can come to terms with the past as well as alter the course for the future.[1]

Restorative justice stands in contradistinction to retributive justice, which is the kind of response that we see in the criminal justice system, one focused upon punishing the offender. Punishment is not targeted upon rehabilitating the offender so much as settling scores; it repays an offense with a bad consequence—an eye for an eye. Mills seeks instead to help the couples to understand the violence in its context, to change the way they think about violence (usually by blaming others), to take responsibility for their part in the escalating cycles, and to feel each other's pain.

On the model of Archbishop Desmond Tutu's post-apartheid Truth and Reconciliation Commission of South Africa, Mills' "Circles" call for public acts of apology and forgiveness to heal the past violences, rather than punitive spectacles, like the Nuremberg Trials, that leave the perpetrators no escape from the shame that often drives them to perpetrate. The object is to repair the harm done and secure the commitment of the whole family to a future that is free from violence, armed with more appropriate tools for managing conflict and stress. "The very process of talking to one another helps family members reconnect and develop a new pattern of communicating when things go wrong."[2]

For Mills, violence is a form of communication, an extreme form to which one turns when other methods have failed. Viewed as communication, violence can then be seen as not a merely unilateral force, as is often thought, but a bi- and multi-lateral force seeking fulfillment by drawing in both speakers and listeners. Thus the solution to the sickened love that is expressed in intimate violence must involve developing more effective methods

1 Ibid.
2 Ibid. p. 210.

of communication than the "No!" that a fist asserts.

Johan Galtung's famed Transcend Method for resolving conflict utilizes a similar approach to resolve conflicts in the public and private sphere. The conflict transformation process seeks first of all to give voice to all legitimate claims and interests. Then the conflict transformation worker raises the conversation a level above all the separate voices, by facilitating a creative transformation of the "zero sum" (win/lose) contest that has caused the stalemate, into a spectrum of creative responses to the problem. The goal is to discover, in the array of potential responses, a win/win resolution which reflects all shared interests and serves all parties' needs. The trick is in the reframing of the conflict, by getting everyone on the same side of the planning table, united by their shared desire to bring the conflict to a win/win conclusion.

Every philosopher knows that any worthy moral system counts every individual as one. However, our lofty ideals about love betray this basic decree and ask us to forget the self in the interest of the other. Our ideals ask us to submit ourselves fully to the dangerous winds of passion, even if submission brings private ruin. These are dangerous ideas to sell to young people on the imposing Hollywood screen. They set up a young hopeful teenager with perilous expectations that can lead to some staggering disappointments in life, and may also lead her or him to suffer—or to dish out—all manner of indignity in the name of passionate love. We have seen in the image of the lovesick Alkibiades that unrequited love damages people to the point of waylaying their glorious destinies and unseating the foundations of their moral character. Having been rejected by his beloved Socrates and shamed for his inappropriate way of loving, Alkibiades fell from the heavenly bliss of love to the hard reality of earthly suffering. Morally and existentially crippled, Alkibiades had nothing (that he cared about) to lose. The next we hear of him, he has disgraced himself and his illustrious family line by public mischief (desecrating statues of Hermes throughout Athens), repeated collusions with enemy states (Sparta and later, Persia), and recurrent betrayals of his city. He was condemned to death in Athens, but met his end in exile on the faraway mountains of Phrygia, where he was brutally murdered.

Plato's account of the young, distraught lover, tormented by unreciprocated love, stumbling in uninvited to the symposium and publicly displaying his private agony, suggests that the trauma of young love may have provided the conditions for Alkibiades' later scandalous behaviors. For all we know, the tragic closing scene of the *Symposium* may have been the direct precursor to Alkibiades' first disgraceful act—the desecration of the *hermai* in Athens. We all know people who were noticeably bettered by the experience of being found worthy of love by someone they valued deeply. We all know too other people who were permanently damaged by love unreturned, love withdrawn, love betrayed or otherwise gone wrong. We know too from decades of research into domestic violence that in abusive families, love becomes entangled with violence, cruelty, pain, and shame, and that childhood experiences of such twisted, distorted love come to be replayed again and again in cycles of intimate violence that rebound across multiple generations in the family. We know as well that childhood victims of intimate abuse may become lifelong partners with violence; they may in their future relationships repeatedly return to the scene of the crime in endless, futile efforts to "fix" the abusive situation and earn the love of the abuser (Linda Mills explains her personal history of abuse in this way), or victims may themselves turn into abusive control-freaks, since their abuse has taught them that powerless people are vulnerable to abuse (and perhaps even deserve it).

These two characteristic life courses of abuse victims demonstrate that love inserts itself at a profound level into the emotional and appetitive aspects of the soul, etching itself into the very identity of the lovers. Love can reconstruct the lovers' essential self-understanding, first through the new blissful vision of reality that promises happy endings in return for faithfulness, and then, when the promises that underpin that vision are broken and love's future cruelly dashed, through the grave disappointment of those promises. When love withdraws its promises of eternal bliss or transforms its tenderness into cruelty, it effects "soul changes" that alienate the lovers not only from each other, but from themselves. *Self*-alienation, *self*-accusation, and *self*-loathing comprise the effects of love lost through tragedy or love withdrawn and transformed into cruelty. Love opens the heart for endless possibility; then agony rushes in to fill up the gaping void carved out in the lover's soul. The lover cannot sleep, cannot eat, may feel paralyzed—"stuck" in grief and mourning—cannot fulfill simple, mundane tasks, but wanders about lost and broken, uncontrollably weeping. She may try to fill the void or numb the pain, as did Alkibiades, with wanton self-destructive mischief, self-abasement, and intoxicants, but these temporary distractions cannot offer permanent relief from the relentless hurt.

Love's loss leaves the abandoned no less confused, suffering, and traumatized than any other tragedy. And as with any trauma, responses are as individual as the person who is suffering it. Individual sufferings are grounded in personal histories, skill sets for awareness and self-healing, and strength and reliability of the support networks that cradle the survivor. As we see in most sufferers of Post-Traumatic Stress Disorder (PTSD), the existential residue of trauma takes the form of persistent, intrusive memories, terrifying, recurrent nightmares, and hypervigilance around social ties, which may be expressed as social avoidance behaviors or controlling behaviors toward others. These will be accompanied by the usual physical aspects of trauma—headaches, backaches, nausea, general bodily aches, pains, and tenseness, and an overall feeling of malaise. Psychological distress symptoms include depression, anxiety, emotional numbing, strained relationships, sudden fits of rage, a sense of helplessness or impending doom. Perhaps the most destructive and persistent symptoms of trauma are those associated with self-alienation: blaming oneself for the loss, a sense of worthlessness, shame, and other indicators of low self-esteem. Trauma challenges core beliefs about who we most deeply are, about our worthiness as human beings, about the trustworthiness of other human beings, about the fundamental goodness of the human world and the value of significant relationships, and about the existence of a loving and caring protector god.

The effects of trauma, including and perhaps especially, the trauma of love, are many and daunting. However, much research has taken place in the field of trauma studies since the "empire" of trauma studies took rise from the British railway accidents of 1866 and 1870.[1] A wealth of evidence testifies to the existence of a broad palette of effective practices for healing from trauma, practices to build up the survivor's skill set and knowledge base so that she may be better prepared for managing the inevitable stressors of human life in the myriad forms they arise. Cognitive behavioral practices can help to reduce anxiety and anger and to overcome the tendency toward social avoidance that often follow the trauma of lost love; they can help break through the self-protective walls that are erected in response to trauma and endure to isolate the survivor and distance her from feelings of vulnerability. Relationship and communication strategies can help the survivor process the trauma and transform her ways of relating. As with other trauma victims, safe, gradual exposure can be key to helping survivors to sort out the trauma memories and to reframe their painful memories as a story, a chapter—and only a single chapter that is past—in a grander and continuing life story.

It is critical to follow a painful loss, the paradigm of which is lost love, with a structured program for healing. Initiating a program for healing is often the hardest part, however, precisely because traumatic loss can leave people as it left Alkibiades—broken and morally crippled, sometimes for the rest of their lives. Many are unable to reach out to others for the support they need for healing, and are incapable of rallying the hope and appreciation for life that would stimulate them to seek out and undertake healing practices. For these reasons, many will go the way of Alkibiades—rushing downhill into personal ruin.

However, the truth is that trauma survived can be an enormous benefit in the human life, if it induces awareness and compassion for suffering others. People can learn a great deal from their pain and loss, and use this learning as stepping stones to build new strengths, greater understanding, and deeper empathy with others. Precisely the trauma of lost love can remind people how precious loved ones are. Love's victim, once healed from the trauma of loss, can arise from the ashes of love with a

---

1 For a full history of the rise of trauma studies, see Dider Fassin and Richard Rechtmen, *The Empire of Trauma: An Inquiry into the Condition of Victimhood*, Rachel Gomme, trans. (Princeton and Oxford: Princeton University Press, 2009).

heightened appreciation for life and for other people, intensified sensitivity to their suffering, and amplified desire to alleviate others' pain. Trauma can open new avenues for understanding and connecting with others, enriching life's meaning, and sorting out personal goals.

Unhealed, survivors of trauma, having connected their past suffering with their past powerlessness, can be dangerous to others in proximity, as they desperately struggle to take the helm of their relationships and secure the power that they understand to protect them from future abuse. However, as we have seen above, once healed from the pain of the trauma, the lover who rises from the ashes of lost love can blossom into a far more compassionate being, deeply sensitized—humanized—by the pain, using their own suffering to connect with all living beings in the common fragility of happiness, the common vulnerability to hurt.

It is critical, therefore, that the traumatized lover develop strategies for processing her suffering so as to turn her ill fate to good and derive some benefit from the pain. The survivor needs a method, a practice, for moving forward positively—glass half full. It is critical to understand the effects of trauma if one is to work to untangle the knots that it leaves in the survivor's body and mind.

Precisely because the mind *is* the body, the survivor is likely to continue to present both physical and psychological symptoms long after the trauma of love's loss is well in the past. These symptoms were entirely adaptive and necessary under threat (and as we have seen, the threat is very real at the homespace), but which have the tendency to linger on long after the danger has subsided. The psychological signs of hypervigilance (where stress hormones keep your attention riveted, scanning for evidence of continuing threat), anxiety, and fear (that motivates flight-or-fight responses) parallel an inner explosion of physical indicators of stress that undermine health and suspend recovery; high levels of adrenalin and sharp spikes in blood sugar levels provide quick energy for flight or fight responses, but they also increase heart rate, supercharge oxygen through the respiratory system and into the muscles, and divert blood to the heart, muscles, and lungs from the skin, liver, and digestive system. These dramatic shifts in the patterns of operation among fundamental systems that regulate bodily health cause host of related difficulties: hyperventilation, overheating, sweating, dizziness, blurry vision, pupils dilated, sensitivity to light, tense, aching muscles, poor digestion, eating binges or loss of appetite, stomach pain, stomach upsets, such as vomiting and diarrhea, sallow skin, and inefficient processing of waste. Primed for quick response to threat, dizzy, sweating, and hypervigilant, we experience an overwhelming panicky urge to jump into action. Our view of the world becomes distorted and reality takes on a sense of the surreal: the familiar seems strange, the real unreal and removed, we feel detached, confused, isolated, ungrounded. We may try to battle this spectrum of symptoms with coping strategies that help in the moment but can exacerbate our problems in a short time—alcohol or drug use to calm the mind and body, avoidance of social contact, or complete withdrawal into the self.

Because many of these coping strategies have a tendency to run on auto-pilot and turn unhealthy in the long run, the trick to healing from trauma is to consciously, actively create a toolbox of healthy coping strategies. This toolbox comprises a set of daily routines that identify the lingering stress responses, measure their continuing effects on the body/mind and on wellbeing in general, and create awareness of how fear and anxiety function to frame future experiences, causing us to fear being alone or to accept, and even become addicted to, pain and trauma (crisis-junkies).

One simple, early practice the trauma victim can adopt to turn the tide of her pain is to consciously put a halt to the negative self-talk that so often lingers—I caused it; it's my fault; I am unworthy of love; I suffer to protect my children; I am incapable of being alone; our love was "meant to be"; I will never get over the loss; I need another lover *right away* to heal the pain of loss; I am losing my mind; I can't live without him; I'm wrong and he's right. The list of crazy talk has endless variations, and every one of them can sound utterly convincing to the wounded heart and the mind rattled by trauma.

For the same reason that negative self-talk is so damaging, positive self-talk is salubrious. Count your blessings freely and give yourself pep talks when you are feeling blue, declaring—

aloud if you like, for deeper existential effect—how lucky you are to have experienced what many people never achieve—a love so deep that its loss calls for mourning. Remind yourself daily: I am a strong survivor, a phoenix, a warrior triumphant; I have scaled the heights of love, endured the fires of suffering, and emerged whole and intact. I am my own best company! I am an example for others to follow. Precisely because the body *is* the mind, changing the record on the auto-play of your mind can have positive results for mental attitude and untangle the knots of stress that have accumulated in the recesses of the body to stifle physical health.

Mindfulness practices, in the form of relaxation practices or insight meditation, serve multiple purposes in the trauma healing regimen. Relaxation practices, which may include simple breathing exercises, counting/breathing exercises, simple body scan exercises, and keen observation of slowed-down mundane routines, such as garden work, brushing the teeth, eating, or washing dishes, can be profoundly healing. Doing anything very, very slowly, with pronounced attention to every detail of the task, can bring deep joy to everyday tasks, while it also reduces the effects of stress, support relaxed states of mind/body, grant a sense of groundedness, focus the racing, troubled mind, and cultivate intense self-awareness. A wealth of research evidence collected over the past thirty years show mindfulness practices to be a highly effective way of managing pain, at least as effective as pharmacological remedies but without the many negative side-effects of the latter.[1] Sitting mindfully for a mere twenty minutes a day and getting your mind back in your body brings focused awareness to the pockets of stress lodged throughout the body. Merely bringing into view the tight chest, sore neck, and painful muscles—the simple act of watching them with nonjudgmental awareness can rather miraculously heal the trouble spots.

Groundedness practice is a helpful strategy when you feel your anxiety rising and desperate, self-deprecating thoughts racing through your mind. When you notice the panic returning, focus on where you are at that moment; focus on being here now. Give fullest attention to your environment. Look around

---

1 Jon Zabat-Zinn, *Wherever You Go There You Are: Mindfulness Meditation in Everyday Life* (New York: Hyperion, 1994).

and take careful notice of the colors, sights, sounds, smells, and textures that surround you. Try describing the features of things around you in the finest detail. Look for their less-than-obvious beauty. Notice the things that are joyful in your immediate presence. Make an appreciation statement: *I am fortunate to be surrounded by*... or *I am lucky to know*... and offer your good fortune to others as blessings. Offerings are gestures of compassion for fellow creatures and giving is the immediate cure for the "poverty mentality" that comes with too much ego-based focus on what has been loved and lost. If nothing else, the groundedness ritual will remove the focus from what you have lost in the past to what the world is offering up for your enjoyment at this very moment.

Another helpful strategic tool to place in your healing toolbox is the journal. This journal is another mindfulness practice, but its content is nothing like that which you recorded in the journal you kept when you were a teen, where you hid your daily secrets out of sight of the judging world. However, the focus in the mindfulness journal is on tracking your progress at healing your anxiety. Think of your evening journal as your anxiety monitor. Describe each feeling state you remember from your day and rate each on a scale of zero to seven, where zero is calm and relaxed; one is mostly calm, interrupted by an occasional worry; two is mild nervousness, which still allowed you to attend to your daily affairs and duties; three is moderate anxiety, where you recall being distracted and irritable, and your body felt tense, shaky or weak; four is moderate to severe anxiety, where you were hypervigilant, dizzy, shaking, and you noticed rapid breathing or heart rate, and tension in your chest, neck, or stomach; five is severe anxiety, where you felt overwhelmed with anxiety and strong physical symptoms; six is a critical degree of anxiety, where you feel panicky and urged into action; and seven is unbearable panic, beyond a manageable level of anxiety, where you feel you must have your lover back or die.

Take the time at the close of your day to record when you felt anxious, nervous, suspicious, frightened, where you were and what you were doing at that moment—away from home, around others, or all alone. You may have felt generally sad or fearful with no clear triggering situation, no reason in view. If this is the case, simply say so. Journaling is not only a comfort-ing exercise that gets the inner anxieties *out there* where they can be clearly seen and rationally reconsidered, but translating our feelings into words on a page reminds us that just as the pages fill up and then turn, starting fresh again, emotional states too are mere passing phenomena—clouds in a clear, blue sky. The fearful, tearful, and anxious moments that we have recorded on the journal page teach us too that negative emotions are a roller-coaster ride, and to see that is to want to get off. Moreover, the practice of paying attention to our fluctuating emotions will help us to make logical connections between the activities we choose to fill our days and the emotional states to which they give rise. Taking account of these connections can tempt us out of our lethargy and mindless broodings and lead us back out into the world.

The trick is not to fight the waves of emotion that follow love's loss. Pay attention to your troubled heart, mind it, take care of it, cradle it in your loving attention. Stay with it, even when staying feels tough or boring or scary or stupid. Sit with your mind/body's panic/alarm system, welcoming its signals, reading its messages, using them as opportunities to know your-self fully, to grow in self-understanding and wisdom. Riding out the waves of our emotions, we build fearlessness, self-worth, and faith in our ability to come back from any tragedy. Watch-ing the passing states of our mind across time, whether during meditation and in journaling, puts the hard moments of our life into perspective. We may have a bad day but we can simply wait it out, because the ups and downs recorded across the pages of our journal remind us that all emotional states are fleeting. They come to be, they stay a while, and then they disappear as sud-denly as they arose. So when love is shipwrecked and all is lost and you feel you have no reason to live, take yourself seriously! Sit with yourself like an ailing friend, take your anxiety's tem-perature, record what you are thinking and feeling, and listen to your heart as though someone really cares—because if you don't, no one else will.

We have seen that psychologist Mark Epstein recommends meditative practices such as these as helpful strategies for heal-ing from the sense of loss that haunts human existence. All loss, explained the psychologist, resonates with the primal loss.[1] At the foundation of our psyches, we forever mourn the loss of the primal state of infant-mother wholeness, when in the awareness of the infant, mother and child were not separate beings but one complete nurturing whole that miraculously filled every need. Primordially, all the universe was *me*. Our mourning for the lost completeness follows us into our lives and sets the stage for the loves of our lives. That is, it sets us up for predictable disappointment. No one else ever did—or could—complete me, because completeness is a myth, a delusion, in the first place. Mother was always other—radically, indefinably other. And so is the lover to whom I turn in later life to fill the void. Nonetheless that primal narcissistic state establishes the paradigm for all later loves. Its promise of fulfillment of fragmented, incomplete self follows us into our adult life and haunts our love relationships.

Why, according to Epstein, do meditative strategies work effectively to heal love's trauma? Mourning our lost completeness takes the form of a spatial sense of lack. When mother broke off from me as a separate being, I was left feeling fragmented, like a vessel not adequately filled. Mindfulness practices shift our fundamental metaphor for making sense of the world. Sitting, counting, doodling in our journals, watching the body breathe itself, we become intensely aware that life—and we—happen not as space but as time. Under the spatial metaphor, we are as Aristophanes' sorry little broken creatures, "questing and clasping" after a unique and irreplaceable other half, who we hope will come along and fill the lack in us. However, under the temporal metaphor, the painful aspects of our lives can be seen as simple events on a temporal chain. Through meditative practices, we can learn to ride the waves of that chain, to surf the endless sea of a fluctuating reality whose form is ever new and fresh. Along the way of this journey, we meet others who ride beside us for a while, then turn aside along their own paths. Whether we are minding our mind in our meditation sits or minding our feelings in our journals, paying attention in the moment can not only heal what pains us but can open our hearts to a hidden joy in the mysterious flux of being.

---

1 Ibid., p. 81 & ff.

CHAPTER SIXTEEN. RESITUATING THE DAEMONIC MEDIUM

I have opened this work with a query about Hamilton and Cairns' sweeping tribute to Plato's *Symposium* as "one of Plato's two greatest dialogues, either greater than the *Republic* or next to it."[1] This praise, I suggested, may sound exaggerated to the Platonically uninitiated, since the *Symposium* deals with a topic taken generally to be comparatively frivolous—love—while, on the other hand, the *Republic* deals with the vital matter of justice, whose critical import is repeatedly confirmed throughout the opening book of this great tome, and then nine more books are devoted to the topic. Socrates confirms regarding justice:

> it is the business of injustice to engender hatred wherever it is found . . . when it springs up either among free men or slaves, caus[ing] them to hate and be at strife with one another, and mak[ing] them incapable of effective action in common. (*Rep.* 352de)

Socrates also confirms at 352d: "[f]or it is no ordinary matter that we are discussing, but the right conduct of life" and again at 353e: "the [definitive human] excellence or virtue of soul is justice." Therefore the reader may be stunned to read that Hamilton

---

1 Edith Hamilton and Huntington Cairns, *Plato's Collected Dialogues* (Princeton, New Jersey: Princeton University Press, 1991), p. 526.

and Cairns equate the stature of the *Symposium* with that of the great *Republic*. How could a dialogue exploring love be said to rival in importance a dialogue investigating how to accomplish the seemingly much grander virtue of justice that brings into balance human souls and entire cities of human beings?

This seems a great mystery until we consider that justice, in the *Republic*, is ultimately exposed in that dialogue as a fragile and precarious balance of parts: on the one hand justice in the city is a balance among the multiple goals and interests of the classes of the state, and at a more fundamental level, justice in the individual soul is explained as a balance among the three components of the human soul—the rational, the appetitive, and the passionate aspects of the soul. This means that to achieve the critical virtue of justice, the virtue that grants our full humanity in both the city and individual soul, justice must effectively organize the appetitive and the passionate aspects of the human being/community under the judicious tutelage of reason. The passions and the appetites must not be left to run wantonly amok and drag reason down with them into the beastly life of lust and cruelty.

This imagery permits us to unriddle Hamilton and Cairns' mysterious praise for the *Symposium* in relation to the *Republic*. The two dialogues are related in the consonant way that love, operating through the passions and appetites, is related to justice, as the reasonable governance of the passions and the appetites. Getting our loves right turns out to be the very "soul work" equivalent of the work of justice. Getting our loves right has to do with using our reason rightly to govern our bodies and our emotions so as to keep the fires of passion brightly glowing without burning down the homespace. The lovers can trace a vigilant path between Kristeva's two unhappy fates, when reason tends the home fires of appetite and emotion to stoke the lovers' shared investment in everyday affairs without igniting the sadomasochistic cycles of violence to self and other. If we can just get our loves rightly balanced, we have a far better chance of embodying justice in our lives, our homes, and our communities. Getting our loves right equates to the fundamental Buddhist task: accomplishing the life of compassion without getting stuck in ego-based clinging. The balanced love that brings justice to our families and our communities has its origin in learning to love rightly.

In this work, I have highlighted the dangers of a wanton love that throws caution to the winds of passion, merges in a dangerous intimacy, and sacrifices freedom and reason to satisfy an insatiable primal longing for a lost completeness. Only where love connects fundamentally with justice, where passion and appetite are reasonably balanced, can a higher love of compassion be achieved that refuses harm doing. As the Dalai Lama argues in his book *How to Practice: The Way to a Meaningful Life*, "Real compassion is based on reason. Ordinary compassion or love is limited by desire or attachment."[1]

Many religions focus on love as the primary virtue and recommend it as the healing remedy to strife in families, as well as in human communities. Does this mean that religion is the cure to the violence that floods the homespace and leaks out into the world? The nineteenth-century Christian philosopher of love, Søren Kierkegaard, explicitly endorses love as the key to just human dwelling. In one of few treatises authored under his own name, *Works of Love*, Kierkegaard explores the connection between right living and right loving. His account offers some curious parallels and important distinctions to Plato's accounts of love in the *Symposium* and the *Phaedrus*. In *Works of Love*, Kierkegaard argues that love has a variety of aspects and he attempts to sort out its Janus faces. He begins his investigation of love where I began this chapter—by questioning whether love is merely a frivolous, romantic notion inconsequential to important concerns such as justice. Straightway, he rejects the view suggested by the Platonic imagery of the wanton ignoble horse that, driven by lust, pulls the whole-soul to its moral doom by pouncing upon the beloved, rather than standing back in awe of her divinity (*Phaedrus* 253c-254e). For Kierkegaard, love is not simply a dangerous and wanton passion to be avoided or forcibly restrained in the interest of the tranquil life. Instead, love is a critical part of the full, just, and happy human life.

Kierkegaard affirms in the opening pages of *Works of Love*, "to cheat oneself out of love is the most terrible deception; it is an

---

1 Dalai Lama, *How to Practice: The Way to a Meaningful Life*, Jeffrey Hopkins, trans. & ed. (New York: Atria Books, 2002), p. 76.

eternal loss for which there is no reparation."[1] In light of my cautious, and often critical, approach to love in the current work, I recoil in culpability as he goes on to warn lovers against us "deceivers" who mistake love as a morally crippling obstruction to justice with its false promises of human fulfillment. We "deceivers" make it our mission, Kierkegaard warns, to heal the lovestruck of their sickness, but Kierkegaard assures us in a passage that resonates Diotima's mythical truth, that the value of love may best be known by its beautiful fruits, just as we "deceivers" who denigrate love may be known by the fruits of our lying discourse—"by the bitterness of [our] mockery, by the sharpness of [our] 'good sense,' by the poisonous spirit of [our] distrust, by the penetrating chill of [our] callousness."[2] Kierkegaard holds up an unflattering mirror for the skeptical deceiver, such as I have played here, who sees love as a potentially destructive force that splits, rather than heals, human bonds.

How will the Christian philosopher purify our Platonic understanding of love as the wayward daemon who drags our reasonable charioteer through the muck of excessive emotion and down the path of wanton and insatiable sexual desire? To expose the crux of my misunderstanding, Kierkegaard will fall back upon the definition of love employed by the eulogists in the flattering opening speeches of the *Symposium*: he will reinstate Eros as a god. Love has a hidden life, a secret identity in the divine. He argues:

> The hidden life of love is in the most inward depths, unfathomable, and still has an unfathomable relationship with the whole of existence. As the quiet lake is fed deep down by the flow of hidden springs, which no eye can see, so a human being's love is grounded, still more deeply in God's love. If there were no spring at the bottom, if God were not love, then there would be neither a little lake nor a [hu]man's love. [3]

On Kierkegaard's terms, the love that is dangerous and de-

1 Søren Kierkegaard, *Works of Love* (New York: Harper Perennial, 2009), Howard and Edna Hong, trans., p. 23.
2 Ibid., p. 25.
3 Ibid, 26-27.

structive is of an inferior type. The love we deceivers oppose is a deceptive breed of attachment. As the reflection that dances on the surface of a lake hides the truth of the lake's source—the spring that feeds it—true love, according to the Dane, is the one that emanates from God, the source and wellspring of human loves. Erotic and romantic love merely masquerades as the real thing, as something divine and other-directed, when in truth it is a kind of self-flattery that serves only the interests of the lover.

Kierkegaard returns to the orator's definition of love as a god, and perhaps his definition can help us to think about why love so often goes terribly wrong at the homespace. Kierkegaard's distinction between a divine love and mundane, romantic, erotic love shows the latter to be essentially a form of self-love. Intoxicated (like *Poros* in the garden of the gods), romantic, erotic love does not use its reason for good ends, but is a wily imposter. Just as *Penia* ("Need"), encountering her beloved *Poros* ("Plenty") incapacitated by drunken stupor in the garden of the gods, tricked him into fulfilling her desire for conception, so romantic love only *seems* to attach itself to a particular favorite for the sake of the attachment alone, but actually attaches her needy self to the beloved who can best serve its own private interests.

This love for the single favorite Kierkegaard names love "in distinction" that goes always astray and forsakes its duty to the more general "law of love" that he says is binding upon all Christians through the law to "love your neighbor as yourself," given at Matthew 22:39. Neighbor love is a superior love, argues Kierkegaard. Though it is "sober and uncelebrated," it "holds itself down to earth . . . [and] like a pick, wrenches open the lock of self-love."[1]

Thus, the Danish Christian philosopher is not so far from the "deceiver" after all in recommending neighbor love (what the Buddhists would label compassion) as a safer, more reasonable, broader love over the romantic love for a particular beloved. Kierkegaard's distinction confirms what we fear: the dangerous form of love that plagues the homespace is not a god after all, but is the daemon of Diotima's myth. The erotic love the poets eulogize, the love against which Kristeva warns us, is the ego-

---

1 Ibid., pp. 33-34.

based love that seeks its own fulfillment, the love that maims and kills in the homespace. Eros is an imposter-love, a pretender that deceives by appearing as the loftier, other-focused, selfless original, but actually reaches out to the other only to turn back to the self, attaching only to *my* favorites, and ultimately serving only *me*. Perhaps that is what Diotima was trying to warn us about when she charted the ascent of this intoxicated madness to the top of her heavenly ladder, only to deliver the initiate over, not to the perfect form of love, but only to the blissful sight of Beauty. Perhaps beautiful offspring, far from the fleshy reality on the ground, is the best that the daemon can deliver. Even this is a higher vision than Plato affords to the raging horse of the *Phaedrus* myth, who loses sight of the beautiful and divine beloved in its furious struggle to conquer its prey.[1]

Kierkegaard's explanation of the fraudulent, self-serving love is helpful for our understanding of what goes wrong at the homespace that renders it a site of frequent violence. At the homespace, it is critical that we learn to love rightly outside personal interests and ego-based jealousies and possessiveness. In our communities and at the level of power and politics, it is critical that we use reason not to further our personal interests or the good of our class or party, but to manage our societies with a precision that balances the interests of all. That is true communal love. That is justice. If we can follow Plato and Kierkegaard in reinstating the divinity of a just and balanced other-focused love at every level of our identity and dwelling, perhaps we can make a healthy move toward eliminating the curse of homespace violence.

Kierkegaard may have his love right, but does this mean that religion is the answer to the violence that floods the homespace? In fact, most religions, and certainly all the Abrahamic religions, remain patriarchal in orientation, which positions them for a conservative politics that maintains the gender role distinctions that keep women and children more firmly in their subordinate social places. Mahatma Gandhi's revolutionary grand vision for social transformation begins with strict adherence to the simplest principle of equality, on the argument that wherever a dif-

---

1 Plato, *Phaedrus* 246a & ff.

ferential in justice separates groups of people, there yawns an equivalent gap where violence rushes in.[1] It is not enough to simply return to religion and reinstate the god at the homespace, as Kierkegaard simplistically claims in his conclusion to *Works of Love*. As James A. Haught shows in his book *Holy Hatred*, religion and the levels of violence in society are directly linked; religious societies tend to be far more violent than secular societies.[2] René Girard rightly traces a common origin of homespace violence with religious ritual, but Haught shows Girard to be incorrect in his conclusion—that a return to the religion of Christianity, the religion that provides a ready-made scapegoat to substitute for the "monstrous other," can free us from the historical curse of that lineage of violent ritual.

Diotima's truth about Love, reported by Socrates in the *Symposium*, posits erotic love for the particular beloved individual as the lowest realm on the ladder of loves. The priestess beckons us to ascend to more ethereal—more abstract—forms. Eros, as it turns out, has a lesser beauty and a secret dark identity: erotic love is really self-love. Love at the homespace ultimately sickens to the pathologies that Kristeva predicts, because, as Diotima's myth depicts, Eros is born from need and abandoned sobriety. Eros is not simply passion that requires reasonable control; Eros is the union of wily self-interest with love-drunk stupor, a union that robs the weaker partner of her characteristic acumen and resourcefulness.

The Eros-driven lover has a pragmatic goal in hunting down her love partner, a goal distinct from the good of the beloved. Diotima's myth, the ladder of love and Aristophanes' comic tale all depict a common tragedy: Eros is not driven by desire *for the other*, but only for *self*-completion. Eros increasingly coils back on itself, as it ascends the lofty ladder, at every rung and in ever more rarified works and ways, demanding *self*-reflection, *self*-confirmation, *self*-reproduction. With time, as Kristeva suspects, erotic love always reveals its deeper truth: *the offspring reflect the creator*. The lover sees himself, and not his beloved, in the offspring they create together.

---

1 *The Essential Writings of Mahatma Gandhi*, Raghavan Iyer, ed. (Oxford: Oxford University Press, 1990), p. 17.
2 James A. Haught, *Holy Hatred* (New York: Prometheus Books, 1994).

Why is violence so frequent a visitor to the homespace? The answer to this mystery resides in the ambiguous nature of the ontological glue that turns a house into a home—love. Love is somewhere in-between the mundane and the divine. As it lifts lovers up to the heavens on the wings of blissful emotion, it often—and happily—leaves reason behind on the hard ground of practical life. Love's truth resides somewhere in-between the *Symposium*'s various tales—its sycophantic speeches, its playful, yet disastrous, myths, its lofty ladder of beautiful ends, and its fleshy example of Alkibiades, ruined by a destructive love. It is not that the eulogists are just wrong, the comic is merely joking, and Alkibiades is simply a drunken fool, while Socrates, the master philosopher has a bird's eye view of love's truth gleaned from the riddling seer. It is rather that love is all the things the many guests, bidden and unbidden, encompass in their homages, riddle in their myths, and exemplify in their lives. Love, like the homespace where it chiefly resides, is an ambiguous and complex entity. Having many and diverse meanings, it is driven by contradictory forces to serve conflicted interests and produce paradoxical effects. Love and home are caught in between an obsessive claustrophobic closedness, which suppresses difference for the sake of achieving a sense of security and an illusion of commonality, and a risky openness, which dilutes its singularity and sullies its sacredness for the sake of a higher ethos of neighbor-love and compassion.

Almost exclusively, when people are mildly or seriously harmed, they are far more likely to be harmed right within their own homes by people they count on for protection, people with whom they are intimately connected, people who profess to love them. The truth about homely violence strikes us as a stunning paradox, largely because it defies phenomenological explanation, because the stranger always already *comes to appearance* as threatening. By definition, by understanding, by lived experience, the stranger is the prototype of the untrustworthy unknown, while the lover represents the ally, the protector, the heroic comrade who swoops us in to shelters us against a frightening and chaotic world.

Ideally, homes are expected to be joyful, tranquil, supportive sites of human dwelling, where people come home to rest from the rigors of their workaday world, where their dreams are met with support and care, not ridicule or disapproval, and where people are their safest. But human intraspecies violence, as the anthropologists have shown, has its origin in the homespace and rebounds across space and time in future articulations of violence. When people have been raised in violent homes, they carry those historical wounds out into the world, into their subsequent relationships, and into their future home-craft practices.

Healing from the trauma of sickly love is critical to justice in the homespace and beyond, because fearful, wounded people are impoverished in their self-esteem, hypervigilant in their love relationships, and power-hungry, knowing all too well the suffering associated with powerlessness. Many years of psychotherapy may be required to break through the survivor's shell of self-protection and heal his core of shame. A rigorous regimen of mindful practices can help him cultivate his self-awareness, rebuild his capacity for a broader, compassionate love, and undo the mythology that happiness is an externally delivered, fragile and fleeting thing, waiting for treachery and betrayal to sever the loving ties or to tighten the grip of homely love to strangle the unvigilant.

SELECTED BIBLIOGRAPHY

Aho, James A. (1981). *Religious Mythology and the Art of War*. Westport, CT: Praeger.

Bartos, Otomar, and Paul Weir (2002). *Using Conflict Theory*. Cambridge: Cambridge University Press.

Basic Writings of Mo Tzu, Hsun Tsu, and Han Fei Tzu (1967). Burton Watson, trans. New York: Columbia University Press.

Baumeister, Roy F. (1997). *Evil: Inside Human Violence and Cruelty*. New York: Freeman & Co.

Bernard, Viola, Perry Ottenberg, and Fritz Redl (1971). "Dehumanization." Nevitt Sanford and Craig Comstock, eds. *Sanctions For Evil*. San Francisco: Jossey-Bass. pp. 102-124.

Bloch, Maurice (1986). *From Blessing to Violence*. Cambridge: Cambridge University Press.

——— (1992). *Prey into Hunter: The Politics of Religious Experience*. Cambridge: Cambridge University Press.

Burkert, Walter (1979). *Homo Necans: An Anthropology of Ancient Greek Sacrificial Ritual and Myth*. Peter Bing, trans. Berkeley: University of California Press.

——— (1987). "The Problem of Ritual Killing" in Robert Hamerton-Kelly, ed. *Violent Origins*. (Stanford, CA: Stanford University Press). pp. 147-176.

——— (1996). *Creation of the Sacred: Tracks of Biology in Early Religions*. Cambridge: Harvard University Press.

Cannon, Walter B. (1978). *The Wisdom of the Body*. New York: Peter Smith Pub.

Collins, Randall (1994). *Four Sociological Traditions: Selected Readings*. Oxford: Oxford University Press.

Dalai Lama, and Howard C. Cutler (1998). *The Art of Happiness: A Handbook for Living*. New York: Riverhead Books.

Dalai Lama (2002). *How to Practice: The Way to a Meaningful Life*. Jeffrey Hopkins, trans. & ed. New York: Atria Books.

Derrida, Jacques (1978). *Writing and Difference*. Alan Bass, trans. Chicago: University of Chicago Press.

Dingfelder, S. (2006) "Violence in the Home Takes Many Forms" in American Psychological Association's *Monitor on Psychology* Vol. 37, No. 9.

Eliade, Mircea (1987). *The Sacred and the Profane: The Nature of Religion*. Willard R. Trask, trans. New York: Harcourt Brace Jovanovich.

Fackenheim, Emil (1994). *To Mend the World*. Bloomington: Indiana University Press.

Fassin, Dider, and Richard Rechtmen (2009). *The Empire of Trauma: An Inquiry into the Condition of Victimhood*. Rachel Gomme, trans. Princeton NJ: Princeton University Press.

Ferrari, G. R. F. (1992). "Platonic Love." Richard Kraut, ed. *Cambridge Companion to Plato* Cambridge: Cambridge University Press. pp. 248-276.

Gibran, Kahlil (2002). *The Prophet*. New York: Alfred A. Knopf.

Girard, René (1979). *Violence and the Sacred*. Patrick Gregory, trans. Baltimore, MD: Johns Hopkins Press.

———(1987). *Things Hidden Since the Foundation of the World*. Steven Bann and Michael Metteer, trans. Stanford, CA.: Stanford University Press.

Glover, Jonathon (1999). *Humanity: A Moral History of the Twentieth Century*. London: Yale University Press.

Graves, Joseph L. Jr. (2005). *The Race Myth: Why We Pretend Race Exists in America*. New York: Penguin.

Habermas, Jürgen (1990). *The Philosophical Discourse of Modernity: Twelve Lectures*. Frederick G. Lawrence, trans. Cambridge, MA: MIT Press.

Hamilton, Edith, and Huntington Cairns (1991). *Plato's Collected Dialogues*. Princeton, NJ: Princeton University Press.

Hardin, Garrett (1968). "The Tragedy of the Commons" in *Science* 162 (3859): pp. 1243-1248.

Haught, James (1994). *Holy Hatred: Religious Conflicts of the 1990s*. New York: Prometheus Books.

Hilgart, Art (November 21, 1994). "The Unscrupulousness Quotient" *The Nation*.

Hobbes, Thomas (1962). *Leviathan.* New York: Fontana.

Kierkegaard, Sören (2009). *Works of Love.* Howard and Edna Hong, trans. New York: Harper Perennial.

Kirk, G. S., and J. E. Raven (1957). *The Presocratic Philosophers.* London: Cambridge University Press.

Kristeva, Julia (1987). *Tales of Love.* Leon S. Roudiez, trans. New York: Columbia University Press.

Lenski, Gerhard E. (1966). *Power and Privilege: A Theory of Social Stratification.* Columbus, OH: McGraw-Hill.

Levinas, Emmanuel (1986) *Collected Philosophical Papers.* Alfonso Lingis, trans. Dordrecht: Kluwer Academic Publishers.

——— (1990). *Nine Talmudic Readings.* trans. Annette Aronowicz. Bloomington: Indiana University Press.

———(1969). *Totality and Infinity: An Essay on Exteriority.* Alfonso Lingis, trans. Pittsburgh: Duquesne University Press.

Lifton, Robert J. (1963). "Psychological Effects of the Atomic Bomb in Hiroshima: The Theme of Death." *Daedalus, Journal of the American Academy of the Arts and Sciences.* 1963. 462-497.

Loewald, Hans (1988). *Sublimation: Inquiries into Theoretical Psychoanalysis.* New Haven, Conn.: Yale University Press.

Lorenz, Konrad (1966). *On Aggression.* Marjorie Kerr Wilson, trans. New York: Harcourt.

Lystad, Mary (1986). *Violence in the Home: Interdisciplinary Perspectives.* Philadelphia: Brunner-Routledge.

May, Rollo (1972). *Power and Innocence.* New York: Norton & Co.

Mencius (1970). D. C. Lau trans. New York: Penguin Classics.

Mikkelsen, Tarjei, et al (2005). "Initial sequence of the chimpanzee genome and comparison with the human genome." *Nature* 437.7055. pp. 69-87.

Mills, Linda G. (2008). *Violent Partners.* New York: Basic Books.

Muller, Martin N., and Richard W. Wrangham (2009). *Sexual Coercion in Primates and Humans.* Cambridge: Harvard University Press.

Nietzsche, Friedrich (1934). *Thus Spake Zarathustra*, Thomas Common, trans. New York: Tudor.

Nussbaum, Martha (1986). *The Fragility of Goodness.* Cambridge, MA: Cambridge University Press.

Priest, Dana (November 2, 2005) "CIA Holds Terror Suspects in Secret Prisons" *Washington Post.*

Rancière, Jacques (1999). *Disagreement: Politics and Philosophy.* Julie Rose, trans. Minneapolis: University of Minnesota Press.

Shils, Edward (1968). *Life or Death: Ethics and Options.* London: D. H. Labby.

Smelser, Neil (1971). "Some Determinants of Destructive Behavior" in Nevitt Sanford and Craig Comstock, eds. *Sanctions For Evil.* San Francisco: Jossey-Bass. pp. 15-24,

Stacey, William, and Anson Shupe (1983). *The Family Secret.* Boston: Beacon Press.

Stark, Rodney (2007). *Sociology.* Independence, KY: Wadsworth.

The Essential Writings of Mahatma Gandhi (1990). Raghavan Iyer, ed. Oxford: Oxford University Press.

Weil, Simone (1976). *Intimations of Christianity Among the Ancient Greeks.* Elizabeth Chase Geissbuhler, ed. and trans. London: Routledge and Kegan Paul.

Zabat-Zinn, Jon (1994). *Wherever You Go There You Are: Mindfulness Meditation in Everyday Life.* New York: Hyperion.

Zlomislic, Marko (2007). *Jacques Derrida's Aporetic Ethics.* Lanham, Maryland: Lexington Books.

ABOUT THE AUTHOR

Wendy C. Hamblet is a Canadian philosopher currently serving as a Professor at North Carolina A&T State University, Greensboro, North Carolina, where she teaches undergraduate courses in Philosophy, Ethics, and Liberal Studies. Her research focuses upon the problems of peaceful engagement within and among human communities, especially for communities that have suffered histories of radical victimization. She has published numerous books on violence: *The Sacred Monstrous: A Reflection on Violence in Human Communities* (2005); *Savage Constructions: A Theory of Rebounding Violence in Africa* (2008); *The Lesser Good: The Problem of Justice in Plato and Levinas* (2008); and *Punishment and Shame: A Philosophical Study* (2011). Her papers are widely published in professional journals, including *The Monist*, *Prima Philosophia*, *Existentia*, *Philosophical Writings*, and *Ethica*. Professor Hamblet is an alumnus of the *Center for Advanced Holocaust Studies* at the United States Holocaust Memorial Museum in Washington D.C. and she is affiliated with the *International Association of Genocide Scholars*, the *Transcend Network of Peace Activist Scholars*, and she serves in the capacity of Executive Director of the *Concerned Philosophers For Peace*. Hamblet is also the Director of the *International Center for Organizational Excellence*, a consulting firm that offers professional development workshops in the international arena in the fields of Organizational Ethics, Corrections Reform, Youth Anti-Violence, and Conflict Transformation.

INDEX

E

education, 24, 49, 50, 134
Eliade, Mircea, 64, 204
emotional hardening, 39
Empedocles, 167-169
Epimetheus, 60, 156
Epstein, Mark, 172-174, 191, 192
Eros, 1, 5, 8-11, 13, 18, 19, 23, 139, 149, 196, 198, 199
Eryximachus, 2, 8, 13, 15
ethologist, 66
euporai, 124

F

Fair Trade, 126
Four Noble Truths, 19, 31, 168
freedom, 36, 50, 66, 98, 115, 154, 165-167, 195

G

Galtung, Johan, 112, 183
Gibran, Kahlil, 144, 204
Girard, René, 27, 72-77, 81, 83, 84, 123, 199, 204
Glaucon, 5, 6
Glover, Jonathan, 54
Graves, Joseph L., 129, 204
Great Beast, 48

H

Haught, James A., 105, 199
Hesiod, 7
Hilgart, Art, 116, 204
Hitler, Adolf, 55, 132-134
Hobbes, Thomas, 51, 205
Homer, 7
Hsun Tzu, 45-47, 203
human nature, 28, 43-48, 50-54, 56, 85, 87, 102, 114, 125, 139
hypervigilance, 32-34, 37, 163, 185, 187

I

Idi Amin, 132, 134
imprinting, 64, 65, 84, 102
industrialized societies, 107, 115, 119, 131
infection, 27
instinct inventory, 84, 85

J

Janus, 29, 33, 34, 40, 87, 89, 195

K

karuna, 19
Kierkegaard, Søren, 195-199, 205
Kristeva, Julia, 144, 145, 164, 205

L

Ladder of Love, 12, 13, 199
Leviathan, 51, 205
Levinas, Emmanuel, 59, 152, 164-167, 205, 207
Lifton, Robert J., 39, 205
logic of domination, 79-81, 83
logical infrastructure, 77
logos, 48
Lorenz, Konrad, 52-57, 66, 72, 84, 85, 205

M

Marx, Karl, 112, 114
Maslow's hierarchy, 131
May, Rollo, 33, 40, 99, 135, 205
McWorld, 119, 124
Mencius, 45-47, 205
maitri or metta, 19, 163
Mill, John Stuart, 106
Mills, Linda G., 103, 135, 163, 177, 205
Moonstruck, 143
Mtu ni watu, 121